CW00920973

GROWING HEALTHY VEGETABLES IN SPAIN

From sprouting seeds to giant pumpkins

By Clodagh and Dick Handscombe

Santana Books

Designed by Chris Fajardo
Illustrations by the authors and artwork for chart of 'Holistic Gardening' by Lynne Godfrey.

'Growing Healthy Vegetables in Spain'
is published by Ediciones Santana S.L.,
Apartado 41, 29650 Mijas-Pueblo (Málaga) Spain
Telephone: (0034) 952 48 58 38 - Fax: (0034) 952 48 53 67
e-mail: info@santanabooks.com

Printed in Spain by Grafisur
Depósito legal: CA-843/06
ISBN-13: 978-84-89954-53-3
ISBN-10: 84-89954-53-4

DEDICATION

To the many amateur gardeners in Spain interested in growing at least some of their own vegetables as the basis for healthy eating for themselves and family, whether they live in a small apartment, townhouse or villa or on a farm or country estate.

We enjoy helping others with their vegetable growing as much as tending our own. We therefore hope that this compendium of our ideas, advice and information helps you grow a diversity of vegetables, whether on a mini or large scale, and that you thoroughly enjoy your harvests raw, cooked and juiced.

ACKNOWLEDGEMENTS

This book would not have been so rich if it were not for the host of good friends and acquaintances of Spanish and other nationalities living in Spain who were prepared to share their memories and experiences of past, current and emerging practices related to the growing of vegetables, and their use in preparing wholesome, appetising and healthy family foods. There are many and for fear of leaving one out by mistake we thank all jointly for their support of our, at times, way-out (according to Spanish traditions) crops and practices.

CONTENTS

PART FOUR — HOW TO GROW HEALTHY WHOLESOME VEGETABLES — 68

PART FIVE — PREVENTING AND CONTROLLING PROBLEMS — 152

PART SIX — A VEGETABLE GARDENING CALENDAR — 186

VOCABULARY AND INDEX — 200

INTRODUCTION

This book and its sister volume *Growing healthy fruit in Spain* are intended to help you grow your own produce from today — whether you live in a villa, finca, town house, penthouse or the smallest apartment. Amazingly, you don't need more than a square metre of space to start. Vegetables don't have to be grown in traditional plots or within orchards. Today's possibilities include sprouters and pots in kitchens and utility rooms, grow bags and containers on apartment terraces, mushroom sacks in garages or cellars and raised beds in gardens and on terraces in patio gardens. Most importantly, none requires much time.

We give guidelines for each and other more traditional methods within this new-style gardening book. A book that was stimulated by a realisation that everyone is being bombarded with propaganda that promotes the concept "Eat more fresh vegetables and fruit to improve your health", but there is no comprehensive book that tells you how to grow your own under Spanish conditions and harvest them when at their best. Also, since organically produced vegetables are more difficult to buy in Spain than in the UK and other northern European countries, we emphasise natural, ecological and organic growing methods.

When we first came to Spain 20 years ago we soon found the climate, soil, seeds and trees very different to those we had experienced before. We have learnt much the hard way in expanding our vegetable and fruit-growing from small beginnings. We started with just a sprouter, a few pots and a four-square-metre raised bed before expanding within the evolving garden to a 20 and then 40-square-metre vegetable plot with various fruit trees planted around the garden for their spring blossom as much as for their fruits. Later we borrowed land in order to expand, initially to 400 and then 800 square metres. We are now very self-sufficient and harvest for our daily needs 365 days a year. Surplus vegetable crops are frozen, bottled, dried, converted into chutneys and jams or pickled along with the annual olive crop. But, as the photographs in the book illustrate, we still continue with some mini and small-scale growing for diversity, convenience to the kitchen and to determine what is possible and easiest to do in small spaces.

Today many of our most satisfying days in Spain are when we are working on the vegetable plot preparing the soil, turning the compost heap, harvesting currently mature crops with a few spare for Spanish neighbours who produce fewer varieties. Then home to eat well al fresco on most nights of the year, enjoying the delights of our flower garden. Perhaps an interesting spread of vegetable-based *tapas,* the freshest of steamed vegetables with locally raised lamb or fish from the harbour and a bowl of freshly picked raspberries. And on fiesta days a vegetable-rich paella. Yes, we both enjoy cooking as much as gardening.

So with altogether more than a 100 years of vegetable and fruit gardening behind us, almost 40 of them in Spain, we are pleased to be able to share our experiences and ideas with you in a way that goes beyond what we have been able to communicate in columns in various newspapers and magazines in Spain and in the UK.

The book is structured into seven parts, each subdivided into manageable sections. The contents of each are practical, designed to be easy to understand and follow. We have aimed to offer something useful to everyone. That is those who have never grown vegetables before, those who used to and are thinking of starting again, and last but not least those with limited or considerable experience interested in improving or extending their efforts. And with special emphasis on the problems of starting to do so in Spain.

One thing we should make clear is that, although this book is about growing and using your own vegetables, it is not a vegetarian book. Rather it is designed to be of benefit to everyone moving to, or already living in Spain, whatever their style of eating.

Quality fresh vegetables and fruit — especially if produced naturally, ecologically and organically — should be of interest to each of the following groups of people:

• Those who wish for but have difficulty in finding fresh organic vegetables.

• Those who already have a reasonably balanced diet based on the traditional, but fast-diminishing concept of the Mediterranean diet rich in fresh vegetables and fruit but who are interested in a fresher and more diverse source of vegetables and fruit.

• Those beginning to recognise that they are eating too many pre-processed/manufactured "fast" foods and that a move to eating more natural, living "slow" foods, especially home-grown vegetables and fruit, would be a beneficial first step.

• Those who claim that their lifestyles are too rushed and stressed to prepare healthy meals but would like to eat more vegetables and fruit to accompany their processed and packaged main courses.

• Committed vegetarians or vegans who recognise that in many retail outlets fruit and vegetables are not as fresh and ripe as they used to be in the best village stores and local markets

• Anyone in the above groups who is concerned that more and more of the the supermarket products, whether from Spain or imported, are being grown under plastic.

Lastly we sincerely hope that our writing efforts will encourage you to grow and enjoy more home-grown vegetables and fruit.

Already we are encouraged. Even though the younger generation is allowing the once-productive traditional *huertos* (allotments), handed down over generations, to wither away, many nearby expatriate and Spanish neighbours who have retired to our inland valley from working lives in towns and cities are growing their own. Hopefully such "new horticulturists" will lead the way in re-establishing the best of the once-traditional Mediterranean gardens/smallholdings and healthy diet. It doesn't matter whether they grow bean sprouts in the kitchen, mushrooms in the under-build, tomatoes and peppers on the apartment terraces or a diversity of vegetables and fruit in their gardens.

Perhaps never in the history of mankind has there been such a need for people of all ages to return to an element of self-sufficiency for the good of their health and enjoyment of life.

— Clodagh and Dick, 2006.

PART ONE

YOUR OPPORTUNITIES AND BENEFITS

There are good reasons why everyone should grow at least some of their own vegetables when living in Spain. Not only for villa and finca owners but for apartment dwellers even if only visiting for holidays. The benefits are discussed in the following sections. They are unquestionable so why not start today even if only on a small scale. You don't even need to have good soil or an abundance of water to have a go. The rest of the book will tell you how.

1.1 THE GREAT OPPORTUNITIES FOR GROWING YOUR OWN

Wouldn't you like to be able to harvest at least some of your own fresh vegetables up to 365 days a year with relatively little effort? The vegetables that you most like, harvested when at their best, and in the quantities you can readily consume before they loose their freshness?

It is certainly possible here in Spain. Not just in a full-scale vegetable garden but also on a smaller or even mini scale in your kitchen, utility room, under-build, garage, or small patio or on your rooftop or apartment terrace. A space no larger than 30 by 30 centimetres is required to make a meaningful start even without having to dirty your hands.

Amazingly, many kilos a year of very tasty and healthy vegetables can be produced in that space. For instance, by first: growing sprouting seed crops in the kitchen; cut-and-come-again salad crops and herbs in pots or in window boxes, or wild mushrooms in special grow bags, or tomatoes and peppers in large pots. Beyond that you can expand your production in a wide variety of containers and raised beds or small patches within the flower garden, cottage-garden style. And of course with more space, time and enthusiasm you can expand to, or in many cases start with, a large vegetable plot growing the full diversity of vegetables. We in fact operate on all three scales in parallel to obtain the maximum seasonal diversity in what we eat, convenience and to gain the experience to pass on to others.

We include selected herbs as vegetables as some by size of leaf can be incorporated as important ingredients in salads and others for generations have been indispensable for some of the more tasty and aromatic vegetable, meat and fish dishes.

Whether you start on a mini or large scale, developments in seeds, organic compost, the design of plant pots and containers, natural versus chemical fertilisers, insecticides and fungicides and mini irrigation systems are making it easier and safer for the inexperienced and experienced to produce good vegetables without too much heartache and effort. It is therefore possible to involve children in the activities to encourage them to eat more vegetables, help them better understand some of their science and environmental lessons and give positive support to "eat well" promotions within Spanish schools.

This book provides step-by-step practical guidelines for growing some 90 types of vegetables in every type of situation. There is therefore no need for gastronomic boredom.

In Your Garden in Spain we included a chapter entitled Painting with Plants to demonstrate what can be achieved by planting different plant combinations using just a few or many of the colours and hues of the painter's palette. There are parallels in the use of your vegetable plants and surrounding flowering fruit trees, the trees being used to provide protection for the more delicate vegetables.

First, the leaves, stems, flowers, fruits and roots of vegetables come in an amazingly wide range of colours. So it is possible to lay out at least part of a vegetable plot to create an effect as pleasing to the eye as a flower garden. And vegetable plants within an annual or perennial bed can create some very interesting cottage garden-like effects.

Second, the diversity of vegetable colours, flavours, aromas, textures, flowers, leaves and roots offer the gardener cook a multi-dimensional palette from which to prepare and display food that not only smells and tastes good but looks good. That can be achieved without the need to rely on E-additive flavour and colour enhancers or packaged sauces.

Overall, growing your own vegetables can be the route to more satisfying as well as more healthy food as illustrated in the diagram below.

There are other advantages in growing your own vegetables. You can eat them at their best season knowing that there is always a new delicious crop just around the corner. And, since your labour is free, you can avoid some of the retail mark-ups on the prices paid to growers (examples quoted in a Valencia newspaper: 772 per cent on leeks, 712 per cent on lettuces, 660 per cent on spinach and 529 per cent on tomatoes). The retail price of out-of-season produce can be even higher, especially if grown organically.

Moreover, you will be able to guarantee yourself locally grown produce at a time when more and more vegetable-producing land surrounding villages and towns is being abandoned or sold for housing developments and golf courses. Many vegetables for sale in greengrocers and supermarkets are already grown under plastic by large-scale producers or imported. The next four photographs show a stretch of Almería's "plasticulture", the inside of a typical commercial greenhouse, a productive organic vegetable plot and the use of pots for growing vegetables and herbs on a terrace (page 18).

Even the greenhouses are under pressure from lower-cost imports from countries such as Italy, Morocco, Mexico and China. If you grow your own, you will be in control of what seeds and treatments you use and avoid the use of GM-modified seeds if that concerns you. GM seeds are mainly modified to improve the productivity of large-scale farming by changing the genetics of the seeds so that they are resistant to herbicides and have inbuilt resistance to specific pests and diseases. We grow our vegetables at a natural rate without

the excess use of water and nitrogenous fertilisers. As a result, we experience few pests and diseases. Any problems that do occur we treat with ecological/organic methods. Nor do we use chemical weed-killers so we are perfectly happy to continue to use traditional seeds. Indeed, we search out heritage seeds which are no longer sold commercially or never have been.

The opportunity is there. We hope that this book will encourage more 21st-century northern European invaders to join us in re-establishing the tradition first introduced by the Romans and Moors that enabled most small town and rural households to be self-sufficient in vegetables and fruit. A tradition widely lost during the last half century as many Spaniards have moved to city apartments. But they themselves are now recognising the benefits of growing vegetables and fruit in the small gardens of their weekend or retirement homes.

1.2 THE DIETARY AND HEALTH BENEFITS FROM GROWING YOUR OWN

Information from government and health institutions indicates that most people would benefit healthwise from eating more vegetables and fruit on a daily basis. Acting on this evidence, many government health departments have launched campaigns to encourage everyone to take positive steps to do so. Spain and the USA are among many countries encouraging people to eat a minimum of five portions a day of fresh vegetables and fruit to ensure the consumption of a healthy input of fresh vitamins, minerals and fibre each day. A number of countries such as Australia go further in their campaigns by encouraging the eating of a minimum of nine portions a day since a greater diversity of vegetables and fruit is likely to include the necessary amounts of essential substances.

SOME APPARENT TRENDS RE DIET AND HEALTHY EATING

• The original Mediterranean diet consisted of fresh vegetables, fruit, herbs and olive oil with fresh fish from an unpolluted Mediterranean sea and rivers and some meat from naturally foraged animals and birds.
• In the past 50 years the Mediterranean diet has been unhealthily modified as a result of many people moving from rural to urban locations, rushed lifestyles, the advent of convenience and snack foods, and pollution.
• Fresh water, vegetables, herbs, fruit and fresh air are the healthiest five ingredients of any diet.

• The greater the diversity and skillful mixing of fresh vegetables and fruit alone or with fish or meat the more likely it is that a meal will be satisfying, healthy and enjoyable.
• Old-fashioned seasonal variations in vegetables and fruit were good for one. One enjoyed what was around at the time and relished the next crops that would be available. Today, when everything is available every day — at a price — as a result of mass production under plastic and world-wide imports, menus can become standardised and boring.
• The best between-meal nibbles are living snacks, such as a crunchy fresh carrot, fresh juicy apple and a handful of fresh bean sprouts.
• The flavours, aromas and colourings of fresh vegetables and fruit are more healthy than the manufactured substitutes.
• Fresh fruit juice from juicy sun-ripened fruit is likely to be more beneficial than juice in cartons produced from imported concentrates with added sweeteners.

Fresh vegetables and fruit are the best source of energy, carbohydrates, protein, vitamins, minerals, oils and anti-oxidants. Unfortunately most of the publicity and writings exhorting us to eat more fresh vegetables miss out two important points: what is truly fresh and where do you obtain the diversity.

From our experience the freshest vegetables are those picked directly from your kitchen sprouter, window boxes, pots, or vegetable garden a few minutes before eating them. The second freshest are those picked early morning for sale at a farm gate, in a local fresh food market or local village store.

And the least fresh? Those purchased prepacked at the end of several days on the shelf, which can be up to a week for vegetables. Although "use by" labels indicate by when vegetables should be eaten, they do not indicate when they were picked. Innovative technology has provided chemical treatments that can enhance the colour, shine, anti-bruising and keeping qualities of many vegetables grown in Spain or imported, whether grown in the fresh air ripened by the sun or grown in large hothouses in an artificial atmosphere.

When it comes to diversity few retail outlets sell the full range of seasonal varieties that can be grown or necessarily the tastiest varieties. Some local governments in Spain are planning to reopen daily municipal vegetable and fruit markets to enable local growers to get produce to the consumer faster than the supermarket distribution channels and to achieve higher incomes than selling at very low prices to the wholesale distributors. However, there is no guarantee that the produce will be grown naturally, ecologically and healthily.

The worldwide Slow Food movement aims to stimulate an improvement in gastronomy by continuing and returning to small-scale domestic production of vegetavbles, fruit, etc.

The overall message is that it's about time we again took responsibility for our own and the family's health through sensible eating and exercise and that growing one's own vegetables can go a long way to providing the basis for this.

That does not necessarily mean having the large allotments or small holdings of many of our ancestors or working in them every spare hour to feed large families. Many vegetables can be grown in small areas — even in one square metre. How to do so is explained in Part Two.

1.3 THE EXTRA BENEFITS FROM GROWING PRODUCE NATURALLY, ECOLOGICALLY AND ORGANICALLY

We have grown vegetables all our lives starting by assisting grandparents and parents, then in our own small plots and by assisting in school vegetable gardens, followed by window boxes and pots in flats and then eventually plots in our own gardens. Having started by improving and feeding soils with natural fertilisers (dug-in green manures and the manures from the chickens, rabbits, pigeons and horses that our families kept) it has always seemed sensible to seek out natural manures rather than using artificial manufactured inorganic fertilisers.

A number of factors have stimulated our desire to expand our vegetable growing without using manufactured chemicals:

1. The desire to be in control and knowledgeable about what products are used in their growing and to ensure that they are friendly to the soil, plants, beneficial insects, animals, birds and the water table.

2. The absence of seeing any obvious benefits from changing over from our life-time of growing vegetables naturally using ecological and organic practices to using manufactured inorganic, synthesised products, other than perhaps producing faster-growing giant plants that would be too large for us to eat fresh.

3. With the better education of smallholders, it is not unusual now to see persons dressed in space suits when spraying their fruit trees with chemical insecticides and fungicides. This is evidence that spraying without such precautions has health risks and the risk of wind drift on to surrounding vegetables needs to be minimised.

4. A nearby smallholder sprayed his vegetable plot with a chemical apparently designed to kill cut worms and eel worms and then flooded his land to get the chemical into the soil. Within an hour the surface of the soil was covered with thousands of dead earthworms, the very things that one needs to attract and multiply to build up a rich fertile soil without resorting to chemical fertilisers (which he used). Even worse, he killed very few cut and eel worms in the process.

5. When we took over our first agricultural terrace, locals tried to persuade us to cover the entire surface of the soil with a continuous plastic sheet and use a canister of fumigating gas overnight to kill off all the organisms and insects in the soil to ensure that we didn't get major plagues and pest problems. We didn't follow their advice and have never had major problems. What signs of disease or pests that have occurred have been speedily solved with natural methods.

6. In the past, before EU regulations required all chemical products to be kept in airtight airconditioned rooms, we would leave many local agricultural cooperatives without buying anything because of the pervading smell and fumes. Now we use them regularly for seeds, tools etc. and notice that the number of alternative products labelled as natural, ecological, biological or organic is increasing annually.

7. The fact that an increasing proportion of Spain's exports of vegetables and fruits to northern Europe is labelled as organically produced and the planned introduction of an EU organic product label.

8. Recent annual visits to the Iberflora and Euroagro fairs have indicated that both major and niche producers and marketers of fertilisers, insecticides and fungicides now offer a full range of ecological and organic alternatives to chemical products.

9. In the Ballesteros Islands off the coast of Peru with their amazing wild life, it was interesting to note the depth of Booby bird droppings *(guano)*. Until the early part of the 20th century it was commercially viable for a British company to clear the islands annually and ship the powerful natural fertiliser to Europe for sale to vegetable and fruit growers.

10. More and more organic produce is being sold in Spanish supermarkets, municipal and local markets, and at the gates of biological/organic growers, although as yet not to the extent as in many other EU countries.

11. Surprise that whole salad vegetables which used to lose their crispness after being on display for a day or two can now be cut and mixed as a ready-bagged salad that stays crisp both within the bag and when taken out for two days. Concerns are emerging that some of the chemicals used to keep them fresh by reducing water losses may contribute to increasing obesity.

12. The extensive popular and scientific writings and EU/national government schemes that extol agriculturalists and householders to produce and consume more fresh ecologically/organically produced vegetables and fruit.

13. Finding that many vegetables sold as organic were not crisp and lacked flavour and aroma after being on the shelf too long in small health shops due to their high relative prices, only one delivery weekly and a lack of meaningful promotion.

14. The lack of pleasure of eating vegetables when not at their best.

15. The amazing reappearance of beneficial insects and small animals after converting land previously worked with chemical products to an ecological/organic plot. Dead sterile soil can soon become alive again.

1.4 ENCOURAGING CHILDREN TO GROW AND EAT VEGETABLES

Worldwide there is growing concern about the inadequate quantities of fresh vegetables and fruit children eat and the possible effects on their ability to grow, exercise, study healthily and avoid obesity.

A growing number of countries have programmes for developing a knowledge of the benefits of vegetables and fruit and some schools include school gardens among their group activities. It was encouraging recently to find that one school took junior students to visit a biological grower of vegetables and fruit (i.e. they only used ploughed-in and composted green manures and no animal manures) as a regular part of the school curriculum to see how things were grown and to collect produce for a weekly mini-market they ran for their parents.

The choice of produce, the understanding of quality standards, the concept of supply and demand, the weighing and pricing of the different vegetables and fruit and working out how much money had been made that week all contributed to a practical real-life learning experience.

However, such initiatives are not universal. It is therefore important that parents and/or grandparents take the lead. The following practical experiences could help young children considerably in their understanding of early science and botany lessons at school:

Smelling things such as ripe tomatoes, strawberries, raspberries, fennel, rosemary and thyme.

Picking and dissecting things such as a globe artichoke or sunflower.

Sowing seeds such as mustard, cress, cut and come again salad leaves, and radishes that will come up and mature quickly.

Seeing the speed at which their own tray of sprouting seeds germinate and grow.

Caring for a patch of strawberries or chives throughout the year.

Drying and painting colourful vegetables such as turk's turban squash and decorative gourds.

Preparing their own salad with their self-grown mustard and cress, lettuce leaves, tomato, radishes, chives and why not sprouting seeds.

Making a refreshing infusion of mint or lemon verbena and helping juice vegetables such as carrots and tomatoes.

Growing a pumpkin for weight or a sunflower for height in a competition with friends and keeping the seeds to see if they can do even better next year.

Learning by doing, asking questions, being coached by an elder and achieving personal success at an early age are the best ways of developing beneficial beliefs and skills for life.

We were both fortunate to have been actively involved and encouraged by parents and grandparents and there were always home-produced manures around to grow all vegetables and fruit without resorting to the use of strong chemical fertilisers. This led us to having our own patches of vegetables and fruit bushes to care for, involvement in school gardens, gaining scout gardening badges and, a most important link, cooking badges. This led naturally to cooking at camps and also collecting, under supervision, edible wild vegetables. It became natural later always to grow what we could, whether living in an apartment or houses with gardens.

For birthday, Christmas or Los Reyes presents, why not purchase books and games with vegetable and fruit themes or mini shops and kitchens that have good reproductions of vegetables and associated fruit included? Although such things already exist, there is a big educational market opportunity for an entrepreneur in this field.

1.5 THE BASIC SUCCESS FACTORS

From our experience there are 10 such factors each achievable with a little dedication and effort. However, if you don't see yourself meeting all 10, don't lose heart — even achieving some of them can be progress towards an improved diet and health.

1. Start small and selectively.

2. Expand when you have the time, motivation, and perhaps family support to make the home-growing of vegetables a priority.

3. Plant what you like to eat or did before being tempted by pre-packed vegetables.

4. Use whatever space you can allocate as productively as possible.

5. Be tempted by the benefits of diversity and try out some new varieties each year.

6. Go ecological/organic from Day One.

7. Recognise that growing healthy vegetables can become more than a mere hobby as the benefits soon impact all aspects of your lifestyle in Spain, regardless of age.

8. Be economical with the use of water and fertilisers. Not just to save money but to grow your produce naturally.

9. Create a sheltered garden environment. Vegetables like humans don't always enjoy the extremes of the Spanish climate.

10. If it takes up too much time, evaluate why. It doesn't need to.

1.6 BENEFITS OF A TOTAL OR HOLISTIC APPROACH TO GARDENING

The advantage of the Spanish climate is that it offers the chance to design and develop gardens for living in rather than looking at through the window, as is often the case when living in cooler, wetter climes. Gardens that match intended outdoor lifestyles in all respects.

In the diagram on the next page, we present our new concept of total or holistic gardening. The outer circle summarises the principal objectives or needs for the development of a satisfying Spanish lifestyle garden and the inner circle the main elements involved in designing and developing a garden to match.

This book concentrates on how you can move towards achieving the top objective through growing a diversity of vegetables including herbs. As you progress through it you will recognise that almost all the inner elements, not only those in the top bright green segment, are important in doing so. They do not apply solely to the development of the flower garden.

Like many we started out with a bare, uninviting building site but with a vision of what we wanted our Garden of Eden or Shangri-la to look like eventually. We concentrated initially on creating a basic framework for a garden before filling in the detail. Once the muddy areas were covered with hard surfaces or stone chippings, one could move around and hedges, trees and shrubs could be progressively planted. Early on, even while we were only absentee gardeners, the beginning of a now-extensive herb collection was planted plus a few easy-to-raise vegetables, so that we could enjoy them while working on the rest of the garden rather than waiting until retirement to enjoy the delights of home-grown produce.

OUR FRAMEWORK FOR HOLISTIC GARDENING

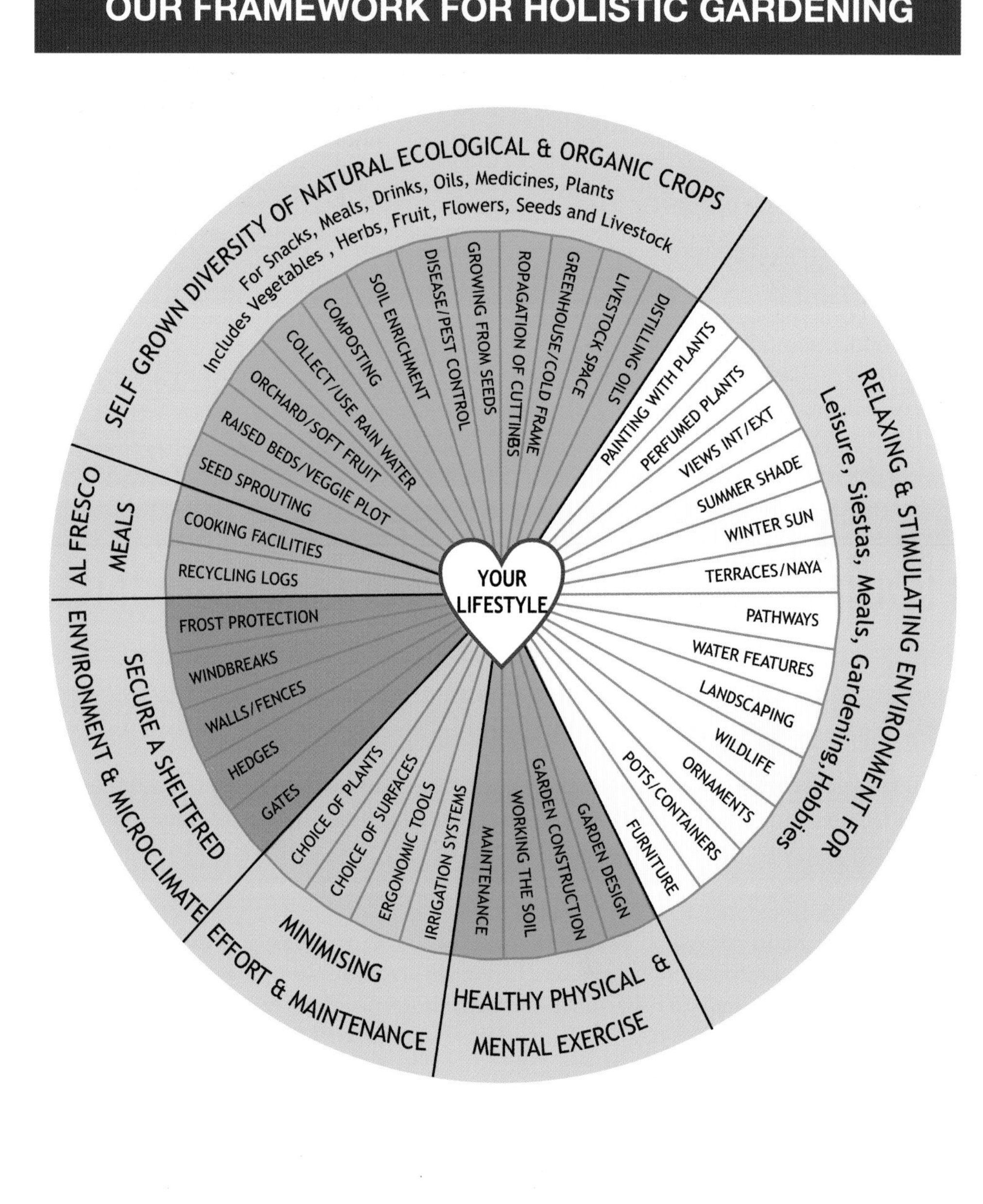

Once retired, we had the time to work on projects like garden seats, ponds and eventually the expansion of the vegetable and fruit garden and the keeping of a few hens, rabbits and snails. These provided light protein to eat with our expanding diversity of vegetables, fruit and edible herbs and also provided natural fertilisers for growing the next year's vegetables and fruit. Some of the herbs were used in cooking, others for healthy infusions and others to treat a variety of ailments. The introduction of fruit trees, herbs and — in the vegetable garden — companion plants helped attract wildlife back into the garden. It changed from being a sterile piece of ground to an energetic, ecologically friendly, restful place to live. Naturally, this didn't occur overnight and we learned by our mistakes, being initially as inexperienced as anyone else in coping with the Spanish climate, soils and plants.

But learning the hard way has enabled us to crystallise our vision of a total or holistic garden for the benefit of others. We reap the benefits daily, benefits related to our physical, mental and bodily health and overall enjoyment of our "retirement". It's a satisfying retirement because it is based on recycling to things we liked doing or had a taste of at various stages of our lives but were constrained by educational demands, family responsibilities, time, or in some cases money from enjoying to the full.

PART TWO

STARTING TO GROW YOUR OWN VEGETABLES ON A MINI SCALE

You will be amazed at what can be achieved in less than one square metre of space especially if you are living in an apartment or small townhouse.

Typical sprouters

Mushroom sack

2.1 WHAT DO WE MEAN BY MINI?

By mini we mean ways of growing vegetables that require only a quarter to one square metre of space. Yes, less than the size of your washing-up bowl or bath. That's all it needs to grow sprouting vegetables, mini-vegetables, tomatoes, peppers, a range of useful herbs and even cultivated or wild mushrooms. Today no one can have the excuse that they don't have the space. So why not start this week?

Within only a week or two you could already be dining gastronomically and healthily on your freshly harvested vegetables — vegetables that have never been treated with chemical pesticides. Additionally, not only do these crops need little space, they also need little time, no previous gardening knowledge, no expensive tools and — most importantly — little water. They are therefore ideal for persons not ready or motivated to find the time required for a formal vegetable garden, and also persons living under drought conditions. At such times mini-vegetable growing is also convenient for those who have a traditional vegetable plot.

2.2 SOUNDS GREAT! HOW CAN I MAKE A START?

A number of easy methods are outlined below. Some take up far less space than a square metre, even a space no larger than this double page.

Each idea is looked at in more detail in later sections. Some are illustrated in the photographs and others within the text of later sections. We have personally used all of them. Some we continue using for fun and convenience although we have a large vegetable plot.

Spiral snail bed

Tyre bed

Typical container garden

Window boxes

Children´s patch

Bath of rice

• Use jam jars or sprouter to produce a range of sprouting seeds.
Young vegetables high in vitamins and minerals which can be used in sandwiches, salads, alone as snacks, in soups, rice and pasta dishes, casseroles, and crispy spring rolls. With a crop a week many kilos of nutritious and tasty vegetables can be produced each year. And only requiring 0.025 of a square metre of space, less than an A4-sized sheet of paper. This could ideally be in a corner of the kitchen or other room — even in a warm airing cupboard.

• Grow a selection of herbs in pots on a window sill, in a window box or in a terracotta herb barrel on an apartment terrace etc. to add to salads, soups, rice and pasta dishes, casseroles, roasts, and to use as healthy infusions. Six 15cm-diameter pots of say thyme, parsley, basil, mint, chives and oregano would take up less than 0.15sqm. That's not very demanding. Roots of ginger and turmeric are also easy to grow in pots. What a way to improve home-made dishes with home-grown ingredients at the end of the bath or on the terrace.

• A window box is also a good place to grow vegetables. Especially fast-maturing cut-and-come-again salad leaves or even some of the mini vegetables that are becoming popular. Window boxes are also convenient for a collection of edible herbs. Again only requiring about 0.15 of a square metre. This idea is ideal for apartment and town houses, even perhaps the office balcony or on the back of your touring caravan. In the latter case the box is best taken inside during travelling to avoid pollution from car fumes.

• It is also possible to grow a few trays of mini salad vegetables on a board placed across the bath in a rarely used, well-lit guest bathroom. Possible crops include tennis-ball-size lettuces, 20-cent-size radishes, 50cm-size beetroots, mixed spicy oriental salad leaves and seedling sunflowers which add a special touch to salads. If the bathroom is dark, a daylight bulb could be fitted to a light fitting and left on for 12 hours a day.

• An old bath can be used as an excellent mini raised bed. If you don't like the appearance, paint it green and hide it in a sunny place behind a high shrub or orange tree as we have with ours. For fun we first grew two-and-a-half kilos of rice. We ate some as wild rice and the rest we had de-husked on a mini mill at a rice museum, using it for a paella together with our home-grown vegetables. This crop was followed first by some excellent carrots surrounded by onions to ward off any lurking carrot flies and then by our current crop of lettuces and broccoli.

• A similar square metre of space could be used for up to 16 25cm-diameter plastic pots or buckets in which larger vegetables such as tomatoes, peppers, broccoli as well as mini vegetables could be grown. Heavy pots can be easily moved around by purchasing the new-style self-watering plant pots with an integral wheel base or by placing the pots on a set of wheels. These are available in many large garden centres or you can use those supplied for placing under butane gas bottles. For a continuity of harvests, plant up two tomato plants and keep one in full sun and one initially in semi-shade so that it fruits a few weeks later than the first. At an appropriate time, wheel the second one into full sun to fill out and ripen the green tomatoes.

• If you have only a small patio garden, the same square metre could easily be allocated to a two-metre-long, half-metre-wide raised bed for the same range of vegetables.

• Alternatives to small raised beds in both patio gardens and larger gardens are tree tubs, spiral snail beds and tyre beds as illustrated on page 29. We first saw the latter two ideas during a trek across Cuba. They were being used in patio gardens and on roof tops to grow a wide variety of small vegetables. Both types of bed provide a range of soil depths for different types of plants and an element of shade on the non-sunny side for those plants requiring most moisture. They can be constructed on top of a concrete surface or rocky ground.

• Plastic barrels or old oil drums, full height or cut in half, provide ready-made, small raised beds with soil deep enough for growing some prize leeks or carrots or a group of sprouting broccoli plants.

• Cascading tomatoes can be grown in hanging baskets and wall-hanging grow bags are now becoming available. A tier of two, three or even four window boxes could be hung one above the other on the wall of a house or shed equally as well as on an apartment terrace wall.

Plant them as illustrated or use the top one for spring onions and garlic, the second for cut-and-come-again salad leaves, the third for herbs that will be frequently trimmed for use and the lowest one for dwarf trailing tomatoes.

• If you purchase five or seven-litre bottles of water, keep the empties. They are ideal for growing young plantlets for planting on into pots, containers and raised beds etc. Just cut the top third off, fill the base with seed compost and use the cut-off top as a cloche to achieve the warm humid micro-climate required to raise early plants from seed.

• Cut off the tops of milk and juice cartons and tape them together in blocks or rows of four or six. Fill them with good compost and you can plant a range of medium-sized vegetables and also herbs. The containers can be placed on any surface in a sunny or semi-shaded position, on window sills and even fixed to a wooden frame to create a living wall. Groups of four or five can be fixed to posts to create "living posts" using vertical rather than horizontal space.

• Do you like mushrooms? If so, spawned plastic sacks requiring less than a fifth of a square metre (only a little more space than two A4 sheets of paper) can be purchased to grow an interesting range of wild mushrooms as well as cultivated mushrooms. The bags can be kept in a spare bathroom, a cellar, an under-build, garage garden shed or utility room.

• Lastly, be creative about what you plant in. Trailing tomatoes and herbs such as trailing rosemary and marjoram can also be grown in hanging baskets and even the large padded bras one sees hanging up in local markets. The pads provide a good moisture reserve. It may be a way of getting teenage sons interested in gardening. We have even seen chives and garlic grown in a bowler hat and leeks in an old toilet. If you live in a penthouse, how about planting up the planters around the terrace with vegetables rather than geraniums. Then you won't have to worry about the geranium moth problem. And a mini start can be made in gardens of any size with just a couple of tomato plants, small patches of everlasting spinach or lettuces in a flower bed among flowering annuals, perennials or shrubs.

The above ideas are expanded in the sections that follow.

2.3 GROWING SPROUTING SEEDS

A. The benefits

Young sprouted seeds are full of beneficial natural vitamins and minerals. These were stored in the seeds to aid the germination and growth of the sprouts, seedlings and eventually mature plants. If seeds were allowed to grow to maturity they would use up this store of nutrients and need to replenish them from nutrients taken in from the soil and air by various botanical processes. So gastronomically the eating of the sprouting seeds is more beneficial than eating the final plant in terms of content and in many cases the taste, attractive appearance and bite.

B. What can be grown?

Luckily an amazingly diverse range of types of seed. The ones that we have successfully sprouted over the years are listed in the table opposite. Also indicated are the very few days required to grow a crop for eating and the several uses for each type of sprouted seed. It would not make sense to grow and eat all at once unless you had a restaurant, but it does make sense to grow three or four types in parallel in separate trays or to mix two or three that have similar growth times. You will soon find out which individual seeds or mixes of seeds are your and your family's favourites and how they like best to eat them.

A. Seeds for growing in tiered perforated sprouting trays, jars or bags.	Typically ready for harvesting by day:	Presoaking is beneficial for the following hours	For use in/as:			
			Sandwiches	Salads	Mixed wirh other vegetables e.g. stir fried	Added into soups, rice dishes & casseroles
Lentils	3-5	12	*	*	*	*
Fenugreek	3-5	8	*	*	*	*
Alfalfa	4-5	8	*	*	-	-
Rocket	3-5	8	*	*	*	-
Onion	3-5	8	*	*	-	*
Radish	3-5	8	*	*	-	-
Mustard	4-5	-	*	*	-	
Cress	4-5	-	*	*	*	-
Beetroot	4-5	12	*	*	-	-
Adzuki bean	6-8	12	*	*	*	*
Mung bean *	3-5	8	*	*	*	*
Broccoli	5-6	8	*	*	*	-
Wheat**	5-6	12	-	*	*	-
Oriental stir-fry mixes	4-5	-	-	-	*	-
B. Seeds for growing in trays						
Broccoli	5-6	8	*	*	*	-
Sunflower	7-10	12	*	*	*	-
Pumpkin	7-10	24	*	*	*	-
Chick peas	5-6	24	*	*	*	-
Mustard	5-7	24	*	*	-	-
Cress	5-7	-	*	*	-	-

*Mung beans are often sold as green soya beans.
**Sprouted wheat can be juiced in a special juicer to produce an interestingly tasty health drink as an alternative to eating it in salads.

C. Where can the seeds for sprouting be purchased?

Typically, they can be purchased in health shops, the health food sections of supermarkets, and increasingly in garden centres. They can also be purchased by mail order from health food suppliers and some vegetable seed catalogues. Try Sutton Seeds, Thompson and Morgan and The Organic Garden Catalogue for starters. Some of the seeds offered by the latter two companies are grown organically.

Their addresses as well as those of other seed companies which include sprouting seeds in their catalogues are listed in section 4.12.

Make sure that the seeds you purchase are intended for human consumption and not treated with fungicides or germinating agents as often occurs with seeds intending for planting directly in the ground.

D. Success factors for growing sprouting seeds

1. Choice of sprouter

There are six types of seed sprouters. They are illustrated below.

a. One-kilo honey jars.

b. A stack of 2, 3 or 4 plastic perforated trays that is manually watered.

c. More sophisticated two or three-tier systems with an automatically timed watering system. We purchased the one illustrated from www.OrganicCatalogue.com.

d. Open-weave hemp, plastic or silk bags/mini sacks.

e. Single 4cm-deep trays either with a 3cm layer of vermiculite topped with a double layer of kitchen towel paper or only with four or five layers of damp kitchen towel paper.

f. A fun idea for children is to make a mustard and cress sprouting hedgehog from a large potato and cocktail sticks as illustrated on page 32.

2. Choice of seeds

We have already indicated the types of seeds that can be sprouted and where they can be obtained. Their tastes, textures and appearances vary so we suggest that you buy a variety to determine which yourself and family like best in terms of mild versus exotic taste, reliability of sprouting, eatability, and mixes of various sorts.

You could work through the total list included in the table within a few weeks. However, if you have never eaten them before, we suggest you gradually increase the amount and diversity of what you grow over a couple of months. Don't be surprised if the supply you kept in the fridge for a special salad disappears beforehand as they are a very tempting and tasty nibble. We find the easiest to grow are mung/soya beans, fenugreek, radish, rocket, alfalfa, broccoli, lentils and wheat.

They can be mixed on trays or in a bag but those with different germinating rates are best grown on separate trays. Mixes can be particularly tasty, e.g. rocket and radish.

3. Pre-soaking of seeds

As indicated in the table many seeds germinate quicker if they are pre-soaked in water.

4. A twice-a-day washing through

• Jam jars are best covered with muslin held firm with an elastic band. Fill the jars through

the muslin with water, shake the jar and then drain off. Repeat this ensuring that no reservoir is left in the jar.

- Tiered sprouting trays are best washed through by first emptying the bottom reservoir tray and then pouring water into the top unseeded tray. Ensure that you do not use more than the reservoir tray can catch. Leave in the reservoir tray to maintain the humidity in the trays above.
- Obviously an automatic sprouter does this for you, indeed it does it several times an hour but the water reservoir needs changing once every 24 hours.
- Woven bags can just be held under the tap and then drained.
- Sprouting hedgehogs need refreshing by carefully pouring water over the kitchen towel paper or cotton wool base.
- All wash water can be used to water pot plants rather than throwing it away.

5. Constant temperature and semi-shade

The best temperatures for sprouting are between 15 and 20 degrees C. Seeds will sprout down to 10 degrees but slowly. Above 25 degrees they tend to grow too fast and mould can become a problem if a strict washing-through is not adhered to. Semi-shade is ideal, but the initial sprouting can be accelerated by placing sprouters in the dark of a cupboard or airing cupboard until seeds show sign of sprouting. A warm airing cupboard can be particularly useful during the colder winter months if you don't have central heating.

6. Timing of sowing

If you used to grow vegetables on a larger scale and sowed your seeds according to the lunar calendar, do the same with sprouting seeds on a day that is good for planting leaf vegetables. This is discussed in Section 4.15. It may prove of interest to beginners as well.

7. Harvesting and storage

As a general guideline start to harvest when the shoots of larger varieties are 2cm long and shoots of smaller seeds 1cm. But you will soon discover when each particular variety is at its best. Naturally you can eat all of the young plants.

Sprouted seeds are best kept in plastic containers or bags in the vegetable tray and the bottom of the fridge. To keep them really fresh, it is wise to place them in a sieve and rinse through with water every two days. If you have produced more than can be eaten in four or five days, the excess can be frozen but obviously they will not be as good as when fresh.

E. How to grow sprouting seeds on solid trays

Larger seeds such as sunflower and pumpkin are best grown in trays of damp vermiculite or perlite with a couple of layers of kitchen towel paper on top. To harvest cut off the stem and leaf when about 2-3cm high.

Chickpeas and small seeds such as mustard, cress and broccoli can be sprouted on top of damp kitchen towel paper in a shallow tray. Harvest by pulling off the towel paper. Turn the chick peas daily to help germination.

Keep the trays damp by spraying with water from a hand sprayer, preferably twice a day.

2.4 HOW TO GROW MINI VEGETABLES IN TRAYS

Some smaller vegetables can be successfully grown from seeds or plantlets in 8 to 10cm-deep plastic trays such as shown in the photograph below. The tray was filled with a damp mix of 90 per cent of a general seed compost and 10 per cent worm compost with a tablespoon of TerraCottem water absorbing/retaining gel also mixed in. Both worm compost and gel are increasingly available in garden centres. The combination of the nutrients in the worm compost and the gel means that we don't need to feed the growing vegetables. When growing this way, it is important to keep the compost just damp at all times but not soaking wet. This needs very careful watering. It is therefore preferable to make drainage holes in the trays used to grow the vegetables and stand them on a second tray to collect the water that drains through.

Trays of radishes, spring onions, cut-and-come-again salad, rocket, beetroots and carrots can be grown from seed. Imagine taking such a maturing tray with you when camping or caravaning.

For convenience and speed, trays of onions, lettuces, beetroot, parsley and garlic can be grown from purchased plantlets. Garlic can also be grown from cloves broken off any garlic bulb. Onions and garlic grown in trays can either be harvested young for salads or left until mature.

When sowing seeds in such small areas, we suggest that you make centimetre-deep holes with the end of a pencil and place two radish seeds, three salad, rocket or carrot seeds in each hole. Obviously not all in one hole! The holes are best 1cm apart. When the tray is sown, pull a piece of wood lightly over the surface to push compost into the small holes and firm. When the rocket starts to grow, thin out two out of three plants to use in salads and allow the remaining ones to grow larger. If more than one radish or carrot seed germinates in each hole, thin out by removing the weaker seedling.

Onion plantlets should be planted with the bottom of the stem 2cm deep and the individual garlic cloves should be pushed into the soil so that the tip just shows. Both are best planted 2cm apart when growing in trays. Trim off the top third of the onion plantlets before planting to stimulate root growth.

We suggest you change the compost in the trays after growing two lots of crops and recycle the used compost when you pot up flowering plants.

An alternative to using trays is to use grow bags which are really nothing more than a covered tray. They are especially useful for growing tomatoes and peppers in the summer and onions, garlic and broad beans in the winter.

2.5 HOW TO GROW VEGETABLES IN A MINI RAISED BED

Raised beds are a convenient, low-commitment way of growing a few vegetables on a mini or larger scale as will be considered in sections 3.5. The success factors for their use are outlined below.

A. Location

Mini raised beds can be located on many apartment or penthouse terraces, in patio gardens or in corners of larger gardens, against the walls of outhouses, or in built-in planters.

For most of the year and in most locations they are best located in sunny positions. However, in situations where summer temperatures regularly rise above 30 degrees a semi-shade position or the provision of shade by a woven plastic tent or old beach umbrella can become essential._

In windy positions shelter can be as important as your watering and feeding. Use spots sheltered by hedges, walls, trees, large shrubs or specially constructed windbreaks.

B. Depth of soil

The minimum practical depth is 30 cms. This will allow a wide range of shallow rooted crops such as lettuces, carrots, radishes, onions and garlic to be grown even if the bed is placed on a solid rock or concrete base.

Deeper beds of 60cms will allow deeper rooted vegetables such as parsnips, Jerusalem artichokes and potatoes to be grown.

An even deeper bed of a metre will require less bending and be more convenient for infirm or elderly gardeners to work.

C. Quality of soil

This is one of the most vital issues. The richer, the more water-absorbing but free draining and lighter the soil the better your vegetables will grow without the need for copious amounts of additional fertilisers. Such a soil will allow vegetables and herbs to be grown year after year with nothing more than an annual enrichment.

For convenience and cleanliness mini raised beds are best filled with a mix of worm compost or dried manure, a good potting compost and some sharp sand or grit to improve the drainage and aeration properties in the ratio 1:8:1.

The number of typical bags required for a one-metre-square bed is as follows:

Ingredient	**Size of bag** (litres)	**Number of bags required for the following cm depths of soil in bed**		
		30	60	90
Worm compost or manure	50	0,7	1.3	2
Potting compost	80	3	6	9
Sharp sand/grit	10	3	6	9

If you have a mini-composter for kitchen waste, mix this in as well.

If you have a large garden and an active compost heap, alternative mixes are possible as discussed in section 4.3.

If your raised bed is to be in the full sun, it can be useful to work in some water absorbent/ retaining gel to improve the water reservoir in the compost.

D. Your choice of what to grow

There are several ways to use your restricted one square metre of space productively.

First, only plant plantlets and fill any space that becomes vacant as a result of harvesting plants with new plantlets as soon as possible. In this way you won't have to wait so long for crops. By the way plantlets are regularly available in local markets, horticultural shops, agricultural cooperatives, and specialist growers, but you may be restricted by the range of vegetables available.

Second, grow everything from seed but concentrating on smaller fast-growing varieties and the mini-cultivars now offered in mail order catalogues. See section 4.12 for addresses. The advantage: you can grow a wider diversity of vegetables. The disadvantage: they will tie up limited space longer than using plantlets.

Third, grow a combination of plantlets and vegetables from seed in your raised bed.

Fourth, grow your own plantlets in pots before planting out in your raised bed. See section 4.12.

Fifth, grow some trailing plants to make the sides look attractive. Possibilities include tumbling tomatoes, a trailing courgette plant and nasturtiums – their leaves, flower buds and flowers can add a special touch to salads.

Lastly, grow a very restricted range of vegetables, perhaps only one or two, those varieties that are difficult or impossible to find in Spain or you cannot obtain when at their best for flavour and freshness. Our choice would be from tasty tomatoes, Padrón peppers, asparagus, Jerusalem artichokes, red high in carotene carrots, as wide a range of lettuces as possible and new potatoes.

The photograph below shows a mini raised bed that was built of wood from old doors — perhaps not the most beautiful but practical. It was initially used to grow new potatoes. This crop was then followed successfully by tomatoes and peppers and then lettuces, carrots and onions in successive growing seasons.

Growing potatoes is simple. Line the box with 10 centimetres of compost and place seed potatoes 25 centimetres apart on top. Then cover with 15 centimetres of compost and, as soon as leaves show through, bury them in more compost. Continue to do this until the box is full. When the plants flower and start to die back, start to harvest the new potatoes by pushing a gloved hand down into the compost. Eventually empty out the box to harvest the remaining mature potatoes. As with everything, keep the compost just damp.

The compost will now be excellent for filling other containers.

Incidentally, the wooden box shown was lined with black plastic to minimise water losses.

E. Aesthetic design of raised bed

While the appearance of a mini raised bed in a hidden corner of the garden may not be a big issue, this may not be the case on an apartment/penthouse terrace or in a patio garden. So choose the materials used carefully. The possibilities are discussed in Section 3.5. If you don't want to make your own raised beds, some garden centres and mail order catalogues (e.g. www.harrodhorticulture.com and www.OrganicCatalogue.com) illustrate and sell very practical frames for mini raised beds. Elegant deep oblong and square wooden and metal

Tips on growing a wide range of vegetables are provided in Sections 4.5 to 4.8.

planters, which are equally suitable for vegetables as flowering plants, can be seen and obtained on www.unopiu.es. Some have frames that can be added to support tomatoes or climbing beans.

F. Control of extra feeding

If you start with a rich fertile soil, most vegetables will not need any extra feeding provided you top up the nutrient content of the soil each year by adding in a bucket or two of a dried manure or worm compost. Exceptions are tomatoes, peppers, dwarf beans and courgettes which benefit from a fortnightly feed rich in potassium/potash once they start to flower. You will find special organic feeds in any good gardening shop for this purpose. See also Section 5.3.

G. Watering

Aim to keep the soil damp at all times. In hot situations it is worth mixing a little TerraCottem, water-absorbing gel (www.terravida.com), 8-10cm down in the compost to create a back-up reservoir of water.

H. Pest and disease control

If you don't over-feed and over-water, you have a good chance of developing strong healthy plants that are less likely to attract serious pest and disease problems. If something does occur, refer to Section 5.7.

I. Harvesting

Start to enjoy eating your vegetables when at their best. Cut and come again salad leaves can be harvested on a regular basis and don't be afraid to remove leaves from as yet immature lettuces, rocket and other leaf vegetables. Young carrots can be thinned, the thinnings being used for salads and the remainder being left to grow to maturity. Radishes need eating as soon as they are at an edible size, otherwise they go hard and to seed. Incidentally, young radish leaves are a tasty addition to salads as an alternative to rocket leaves. Eat courgettes when they are small and most delicious. Tomatoes and peppers are best harvested when fully ripe. A delight rarely achieved with supermarket alternatives. By trial and error you will soon find out which vegetables you like to grow and at what size you prefer to eat them.

J. Summer shading

If your raised bed dries out too quickly in the summer sun, fix a shade of open-weave windbreak material or alternatively stick an old umbrella in the centre of the raised bed during the day.

2.6 HOW TO GROW VEGETABLES IN CONTAINERS

As indicated in Section 2.2, almost any container can be used to grow vegetables. Some are more aesthetic than others but their appearance can be improved by painting them, growing trailing plants over the sides or placing pots of flowering plants in front.

The success factors are no different to those for mini raised beds as a container is nothing more than a very small raised bed. But the following guidelines will also help you make a success of container grown vegetables.

a. Mix in some TerraCottem gel into the compost halfway down the container. This water absorbing/retaining gel will help maintain a water reservoir in the hottest weather.

b. Ensure that there is a drainage hole in the bottom of all containers to prevent waterlogging and place small containers on drip trays.

c. Larger containers can also be placed on purpose-made wheels or gas bottle wheel bases to enable them to be moved around.

d. Keep containers against a west or east-facing wall if you live in a sun trap during the hottest months of July and August.

e. Ensure that you plant vegetables in containers with a minimum of 30 centimetres of soil.

f. In general grow one variety of vegetable in small containers and a mix in larger ones. The diversity of what can be grown in a mix of containers in less than one square metre is amazing. In the photograph on the previous page the crops growing in the pots were onions, garlic, multiplier onions, carrots, beetroot, mixed oriental salad leaves, peas, beans, courgettes, nasturtiums, tomatoes, peppers and herbs. The central tub was started off in January covered with a plastic sheet raised over wire hoops to create a mini greenhouse. An umbrella was added later to provide midday shade.

g. Keep the outsides of containers clean by an occasional wash with soap and water or a pressure hose.

If the idea of growing vegetables in containers appeals to you, be creative in what you use. In addition to the obvious large plant pots, tree tubs and empty large paint containers, we have seen vegetables growing in an amazing and unusual range of containers. They have included plastic clothes and toy storage boxes, old wheelbarrows and prams, old water jugs and tin baths, redundant life-raft covers, holed glass-fibre dinghies, jacuzzi shells, chimney pots and lengths of large diameter plastic tubing, the body of a rusting open-topped car and back of a truck and even an old bowler hat. In other words you can use anything that can contain 30 centimetres or more of a good compost mix. To economise on compost and reduce their weight, deeper containers can be partly filled with scrap polystyrene foam or empty water bottles.

As discussed in Section 3.2, a collection of containers could be used to expand your vegetable growing way beyond one square metre.

2.7 GROWING HERBS IN POTS, BARRELS OR WINDOW BOXES

We include herbs as vegetables as the leaves and in some cases the flowers can be incorporated into raw salads to achieve an interesting diversity of appetising tastes, smells, colours, textures and bite as well as put to general culinary and health uses. As with other vegetables, they can be grown in a wide range of containers. The only constraint being the depth of soil required and the size of the root ball necessary for a healthy plant. The table below illustrates the possibilities.

TYPE OF HERB	TYPICAL CONTAINERS FOR SUCCESSFUL GROWING			
	Flower pot	**Window Box**	**30 cm-diameter container**	**Mini raised bed**
Basil, large-leaved	*	*		
Borage		*	*	
Chives	*	*		
Dill	*	*	*	
Fennel			*	*
Marjoram	*	*		
Mints	*		*	*
Parsley	*	*		
Purslane		*	*	*
Rosemary			*	*
Pineapple sage			*	*
Tarragon	*		*	
Thyme	*	*		

The success factors for growing herbs in the above type of containers are:

a. Perennials like full sun but semi-shade is preferable during the summer to stop them drying out quickly. Keep annuals and biennials in shady conditions during the hottest days to prevent them from drying out and being burnt by the sun.

b. A similar compost mix as outlined in Section 2.5 for vegetables but with 10 per cent extra sand or grit added.

c. Keep damp at all times.

d. Regular trimming to eat stimulates new growth and well-shaped non leggy plants.

A useful collection of herbs can be grown in a terracotta herb barrel similar to the ones designed for growing strawberries.

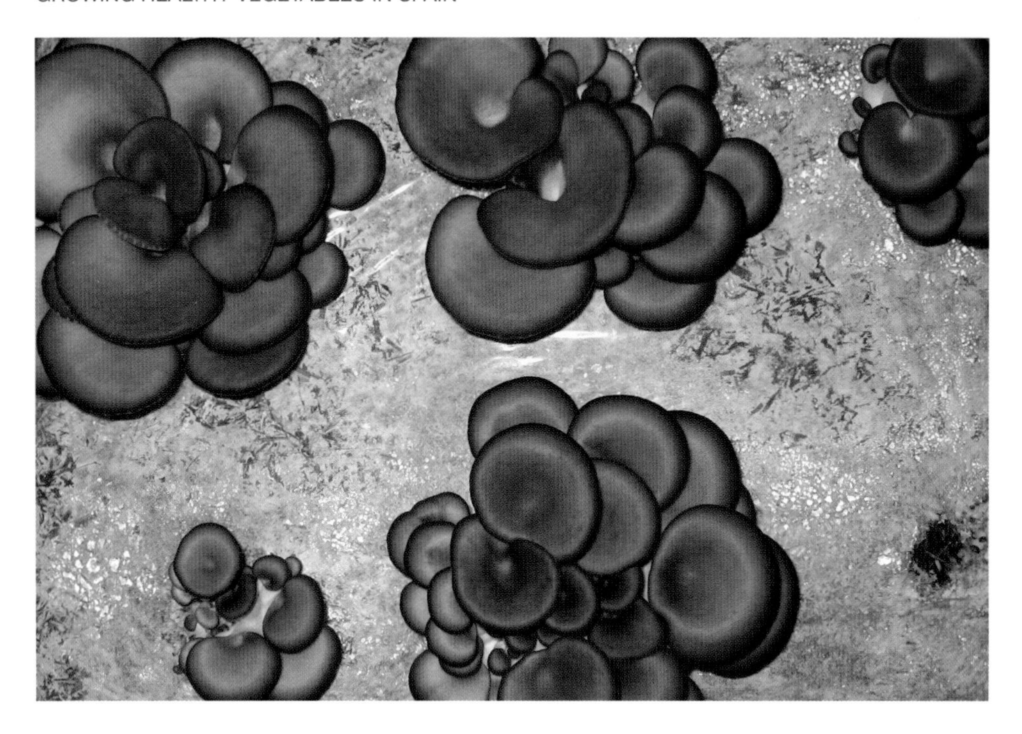

2.8 GROWING MUSHROOMS IS EVEN EASIER

Various claims are made for the nutritional and preventive medicinal properties of the various types of cultivated and edible wild mushrooms. However, many gardeners are not sufficiently knowledgeable about the varieties that are safe — or dangerous — to eat to join local Spaniards in their autumn hunt for *setas* (wild mushrooms). In any case good hunting grounds are kept a secret or controlled in some areas of Spain. Luckily, there is an easy solution which is becoming increasingly popular. Many varieties can easily be grown on a small scale in one's garage, cellar or utility room using specially prepared plastic-covered, spawn-impregnated blocks. Each block is about 35cm by 45cm so takes up little space. The blocks can be purchased in many agricultural cooperatives, animal feed (pienso) warehouses or garden centres. We have seen the following varieties of mushrooms for sale.

• Cultivated mushrooms *(champiñones)* that are best grown in a dark cellar, under build or garage.

• Wild mushrooms *(setas)* in the following varieties: *shitake de salud, níscalo, boleto, seta de chopo* and *seta de cardo*. These are best grown inside with some light, but not direct sunlight, in a utility room or garages with windows.

The optimum temperatures are between 10 and 25 degrees, but they will grow at down to 3 degrees. From our experience there is an advantage in growing at a lower temperature as the crops mature more slowly and one doesn't get a massive crop all at once. A single block can produce up to 15 to 20 kilos over several months and all you need to do is to tear a few holes in the top of the bag and water or not water according to the instructions for each type of mushroom. If you have too many at any one time, they can be made into soup and frozen or dried for later use, as explained in Section 4.17.

If you have difficulty in tracing the mushroom bags, try contacting one of the following to find out about local distributors.

- Cultisett (cultisett@hotmail.com).
- Semillas Hortiflor S.L. (tel. 96-127-5987).

PART THREE

EXPANDING TO A VEGETABLE PLOT OR WHAT?

From the coastal plain to the high mountain valleys there are many practical and productive possibilities.

3.1 WHAT ARE THE VIABLE OPTIONS?

As an elderly Spanish friend said when we first started our vegetable plot: "If there is deep soil, manure and water anything will grow in Spain. The sun does the rest." How right he was. It was already the main message in 1792 when the book *Lecciones Prácticas de Agricultura y Economía* by Vicente del Seixo was published.

Whether you purchase a new property or a long-neglected finca, the extent of weed growth especially after rain will soon tell you whether you have deep, good soil.

A large patch of nettles indicates that at least one part of the land is high in nitrogen and a good place to start a vegetable plot. Likewise, if deep-rooted herbs and weeds grow between large rocks on a hillside, why not vegetables in the future? However, if heavy rain only uncovers more builders' rubble, you know you have a problem. But don't despair; there are several ways of growing large quantities of vegetables if you only have shallow soil or solid bedrock. Each is more practical than using a pneumatic drill to prepare planting holes. For instance, a large collection of containers, large raised beds or a "ten-tub" vegetable garden, our long-term plan when too old to tend our large vegetable plot. Each of these can be fitted into any garden and are also viable options for penthouse and apartment terraces and patio gardens.

If you purchase an old farm, you may be in real luck. Around the house there may only be a few fruit trees desperately needing pruning and old fig and oak trees. It's quite likely that hens scratched around and sheltered here along with goats for more than a century or more. And a mule was probably tied to the oak tree for much of the day. These are ideal spots for turning soil to start to grow vegetables organically from day one, as friends found out. Packets of squash and pilgrim gourd seeds were sown for fun until they had time to get down to vegetable gardening seriously. One squash plant produced a hundred fruits and when we saw the pilgrim gourds some were more than a metre long, hanging 15 metres up from the oak tree's highest branches. Since then our friends have developed an enviable cottage-style vegetable plot in the dappled shade of the trees.

Equally, gardens on rivers' ancient flood plains often have excellent soils for traditional vegetable plots although they may suffer winter frosts.

Before the advent of tourist hotels and apartment blocks market gardens existed in much of the Mediterranean and Canary Islands' coastal plains and still do in a few places. We recently found, sandwiched between two blocks of flats, a small vegetable plot of only 100 square metres overflowing with a wide diversity of vegetables. The peppers, tomatoes and beans were in full sun to ripen them and lettuces, spinach etc. were in the dappled shade of lemon and orange trees to protect them from the hottest hours of the sun.

So anything and everything is as possible on a larger scale, as it is on a mini scale. The only constraints to your larger-scale vegetable growing will be the space you have, the water available, the time you and other members of the family are willing to allocate to growing the family's fresh vegetables or the budget you have for employing a gardener to help. In the sections that follow we will consider eight practical options and help you decide what is for you.

3.2 JUST EXPANDING THE NUMBER AND SIZE OF CONTAINERS

In section 2.6 we described the wide range of containers we have used or seen used to grow vegetables. The obvious way to expand is therefore by using more and bigger containers. The big advantage of container gardening is that it's ideal if you have a garden with no soil but only bedrock under a shallow layer of rubble.

Several tiers of window boxes on walls, lines or groups of small containers, or one or two larger containers such as planter troughs, or 70 to 100cm-diameter plastic tubs (the type used in nurseries for large trees) can provide several metres of growing space. You can aim for a neat set-up with identical matching containers where you are concerned about the aesthetical appearance of your container garden. On the other hand in a wild cottage-type garden or hidden yard you might accept and use any container and make a virtue of the eccentricity.

Containers can be disguised by:

a. plants such as cascading tomatoes, peas, dwarf beans, cucumbers and nasturtiums hanging down the sides.

b. plants such as onions, leeks, herbs, Padrón peppers growing upwards from smaller pots alongside.

If you have groups of pots in the garden, especially in a cottage-style garden, the containers can be stood on the soil or even be partly buried to help retain moisture. However, it is preferable to place containers on square, round or oblong trays on terraces. A large tray for an entire group of containers can be easily constructed from four pieces of wood and heavy-grade black plastic sheeting or a plastic pond-liner. This could be filled with a water-absorbing compost.

The only constraints on growing in containers is the space you are willing to allocate, and the number of suitable containers you are able to collect. The more containers the longer your daily watering and weekly feeding will take whether using a watering can or hosepipe, so it makes sense to install a drip watering system. See Section 4.16.

The table below indicates the easiest crops to grow in different-sized containers. The full range of vegetables that can be grown in Spain and how to grow them is covered in Part Four.

WHAT VEGETABLES ARE AMONG THE EASIEST TO GROW IN CONTAINERS OF VARIOUS TYPES?

A 25cm diameter pots or window boxes	B 50cm pots or square containers	C 80 to 120cm tubs or planters
* Cut-and-come-again salad leaves * Oriental salad leaves * Onions * Garlic * Radishes * Tumbling tomatoes * Mini beetroot * Ginger * Rocket * Small herbs	All A-plus * Tomatoes * Peppers * Aubergines * Broccoli * Leeks * Carrots * Courgettes * Peas * Globe artichokes * Large herbs	All of A and B plus * Lettuces * Spinach, Swiss chard * Dwarf beans * Climbing beans * Squash * Melons * Asparagus * Potatoes * Jerusalem artichokes * A collection of herbs

One advantage of using containers of the above sizes is that in cold areas they could be housed from November to May under a raised sliding or permanent swimming pool cover, in a glazed-in covered area or at any time of year in an underbuild or garage in front of a south-facing window.

Section 3.9 describes a special evolutionary idea developed from the use of tree tubs, one of the most useful containers available.

3.3 A TRADITIONAL VEGETABLE PLOT

A vegetable plot is nothing more than an area allocated to growing vegetables in the ground within an overall garden design. For practical purposes we segregate this from an allotment which is on a piece of land outside the garden. The latter is discussed in the next section 3.4.

The size of a useful vegetable plot can be anything from 20 to several hundred square metres. The size chosen depending on the following factors.

a. The depth and quality of soil you have. If the top soil over bed rock is less than 30 centimetres, consider one of the other alternatives such as containers, raised beds or "ten tubs". If there is soil, this can be enriched as outlined in Section 4.3.

b. The availability of water for irrigating the plot. If in short supply during the summer, it is best to focus your vegetable growing on the period from the first autumn rains through to the spring.

c. The hours that you and family are willing to work on the vegetable plot.

A small 20-square-metre plot should not require more than say a quarter of an hour a day on average while 200 to 400 metres may require an hour or more a day, depending on what you decide to grow and the amount of weed growth in your area. You can include the vegetable plot as one of your gardener's tasks.

d. Whether you plan to grow just a few speciality vegetables or attempt to grow all the family's needs.

Typically vegetable plots are oblongs or squares but there is no reason why they cannot be circular or oval. In all cases a round or square herb garden could be accommodated in

the centre perhaps with a central fountain. Be creative in ensuring that your vegetable plot is one of the highlights of your Spanish garden.

In general, a sunny situation is best, but especially in the southern provinces and Canary Islands it is helpful to have shade on part of the plot during the hottest part of the day. If not, the more tender vegetable plants such as lettuces can wilt and go to seed faster than necessary. Shade can be provided by the shadow of your house, fences, woven plastic screens, woven plastic shades on overhead wires and fruit trees including a row of cordons around the plot. Fences and fruit trees can also protect the plot to some extent from the impact of hot or cold drying winds.

These are the ideal conditions, something we originally had on a small 40-square-metre plot in the garden before we took on an allotment (huerto) along the lines of the next section. This is open to all weathers 300 metres above sea-level, but by taking precautions as outlined in part four and five we grow an excellent range of vegetables throughout the year.

If you are an absentee gardener, locate your vegetable plot against the west side of the house to reduce the direct sun as much as possible and install a drip watering system. If you plant Brussels sprouts in September, they may be ready for your Christmas visit. And the benefit is that they will grow more slowly than in full sun and be small and tight, which many prefer to larger more open ones. When you come out in the summer, you can plant a few tomatoes and peppers in the sunniest corner or grow them in containers on the south side of the house.

A combination of styles of vegetable growing will be the best solution for many gardeners in Spain.

Don't wait until the rest of the garden is laid out and fully planted before starting a vegetable plot. Why not make it the first part of the garden you establish so that you can enjoy fresh vegetables while you work on the rest of the garden?

3.4 A LARGER-SCALE PLOT

If you don't have sufficient land around the house for a reasonably sized vegetable plot, you could consider purchasing or negotiating the loan of a traditional huerto. That is a piece of horticultural/agricultural land outside your village or town, typically a *hanegada* in area. A *hanegada* (a measure used in the Valencia region) is 833.33 square metres, or one-twelfth of a hectare, and therefore a big step to take since it will probably require one or two hours' work a day on average depending on how fastidious you are about weeds. However, you could start by using half and expand over a number of years and by planting fruit trees and bushes as well as vegetables. You would certainly have the space to keep the family totally sufficient in vegetables 365 days a year.

There are likely to be four main issues to deal with:

· The plot may be unfenced and open to entry by wild animals or hunters — also to thieves, although we have only once had a problem. It may be therefore worth having the land fenced before you do anything.

· The land may not have been worked for some years and therefore require a total clean-off and burning of old crops and weeds, followed by a deep ploughing and harrowing before you can start to plan and plant your large vegetable plot and mini orchard.

· The previous owner or tenant may have used chemical fertilisers, insecticides, fungicides and herbicides in a major way. So, if you want to produce your vegetables naturally, ecologically and organically, you will need to enrich the soil as described in Section 4.3 before planting anything and then immediately start to work the land in a natural/ecological/organic manner as described in Section 1.4. The characteristics of a good and poor nano climate for growing your crops is described in Section 3.10.

· The *huerto* may have an open-channel irrigation system originally installed by the Moors, as is ours. This means that the only way to water your plot will be by flooding the whole expanse and by having a few barrels topped up for watering and feeding young plants with a watering can.

If you are prepared to cope with the above, we suggest you start off as follows (the photographs illustrate each of the steps):

a. Clean off the land and burn off all the rubbish. Mattocks and double-edged hoes are the best tools for the job.

b. If it hasn't rained for some time, arrange to flood the entire plot and then leave it for two weeks.

c. Arrange for a villager who has a small tractor to deep plough and then harrow the land for you with a 10-day gap between the two operations or arrange for him to do the ploughing and you follow up with a rotovator.

d. Divide the plot into five-metre-wide strips and raise 25cm-high banks between each strip, ensuring that each strip can be fed by an inlet from the channelled watering system. If there are insufficient inlets, it is not difficult to fit extras. The raising of the banks between the planting strips and the later levelling of the soil between is best done with a large serrated rake as illustrated.

e. Decide what crops you will grow during the first growing season (that is autumn/winter or spring/summer) and what permanent crops you plan such as asparagus, globe and Jerusalem artichokes, herbs (especially comfrey which will be an excellent source of natural fertilisers once you get going), raspberries and other soft fruit, vines and possibly fruit trees.

f. Work out a crop rotation system (see Section 5.6) and layout for the *huerto* recognising that some crops will require more nutrients than others.

g. Enrich the soil as explained in Section 4.3.

h. Level the soil between all the ridges attempting to create a slight fall from the water entry end to the far end of each strip.

i. Before doing anything else, do a trial flooding to check that the land in each strip slopes slightly downwards from the water entry end to ensure that water will flow within a few minutes from end to end. If it doesn't, do some more raking of earth after allowing the land to dry out for a week.

You are now ready to start to sow and plant your plot. Part Four will tell you how, vegetable by vegetable.

We grow a row of comfrey around the edge of our plot. We have achieved this by splitting the plants from our original seven small cuttings each year. We now have several hundred plants. The rows not only ensure that we have a good supply for preparing natural fertilisers but act as a first line of defence against snails, which gorge on their leaves.

3.5 RAISED BEDS

A raised bed is an elevated area of deep soil built up within four retaining walls to allow it to be worked with less bending and normally filled with an optimum soil/compost/manure mix.

There are three basic types:

- A four-sided box constructed so that soil can be worked from all sides without walking on it.
- A three-sided box built onto an existing wall.
- A narrow terrace on a sloping site.

The workable dimensions are as follows:

Retaining wall/soil height

a. A minimum height of 30cm which will provide a depth of soil sufficient for the roots of most vegetable plants.

b. A maximum height of 70 to 80cm to allow the bed to be worked without much bending and also from a stool, chair or wheelchair. The most comfortable height will depend on the height of the person or persons who will be working the raised bed.

c. Any intermediate heights depending on the materials you have available for building the walls and the amount of good soil/compost/manure available. Some popular materials for building the retaining walls are considered in the table opposite.

Width of beds

a A maximum width of 1.5m if the layout of your raised bed/beds will allow you to work from both sides.

b. A maximum width of 70 to 80cm if the raised bed is against a wall or hedge which will only allow it to be worked from one side. If you build raised beds any wider you will need to walk on the soil which will consolidate it and defeat the reason for building the raised beds in the first place.

Length of beds

The length of a raised bed can be anything from one metre to 20 metres or more. However it may be more practical to design a layout with several shorter beds, Allow one-metre-wide paths to accommodate a wheelbarrow or wheelchair.

SOME POSSIBLE MATERIALS FOR CONSTRUCTING THE RETAINING WALLS OF RAISED BEDS

Material	Advantages	Disadvantages
1. Railway sleepers	Can be aesthetic Speedy construction Comfortable to kneel or lean on Long-lasting	Wide so reduces working soil area Wood preservatives can leach out unless lined with heavy-grade plastic sheeting
2. Long logs	Inexpensive Can blend into rural gardens No loss of soil surface	Need treating to prolong life Need plastic lining to prevent leaching out and water run-off
3. Discarded old wooden doors or panels	As above	Not long-lasting Size restricted by size of doors and panels Not always aesthetic
4. Dry stone walls	Attractive Best for low raised beds Relatively easy to build Can grow herbs in wall	Rough on knees and arms when working Need lining with plastic sheeting to prevent water run-off Tall walls a skilled task to achieve stability
5. Cemented stone	Attractive Good for low and high raised beds Reasonably speedy to build More stable than 4 above	A permanent feature Need drainage pipes to prevent build-up of water pressure
6. Aggregate/cinder blocks	Quick to build Narrow blocks available for building walls up to 40cm	Not aesthetic unless rendered Permanent feature Wide blocks can reduce workable soil area
7. Bricks	Can be selected to blend in Can look professional Narrow wall maximises	Urban versus rural appearance Permanent feature
8. Peat blocks	Natural looking Can grow herbs in wall	Can erode Can speed-drying out of soil in summer

The advantages of raised beds are:

a. You do not need to walk on the soil. This means you can use every square centimetre for growing crops and the soil will not be compacted by your feet.

b. They can be filled with a light soil/sand/compost/manure mix which is fertile, well-draining, easy to work and unlikely to be compacted by heavy rains followed by hot baking sun. This is discussed in detail in Section 4.3.

c. The paths between and around the beds can be clear of weeds and mud. They can either be pointed rock slabs or 5cm of stone chippings laid over black plastic sheeting.

d. You can use them in a garden which has no topsoil and even on solid rock or a previously concreted area.

e. A drip or porous pipe irrigation system can be easily set up.

f. Anything including potatoes and Jerusalem artichokes can be grown in soil depths of 40cm or more.

g. Spreading vegetables such as courgettes, cucumbers, trailing tomatoes, capers and nasturtiums can be cascaded down the outside of the walls to reduce the space taken up on the top of the bed.

h. It is easy to install tunnel cloches made to fit the beds for winter plant protection and summer shading for leaf crops that can wither in the sun.

i. Plantlets can be conveniently raised under cloches if you have the room. But, as with all small-scale vegetable growing, maximum productivity will be achieved by constantly filling any space freed when harvesting crops with new plantlets or fast maturing crops.

j. They are easy to extend if you have the space.

k. A number of raised beds could be hidden away in various parts of the garden if you do not want a large dedicated area.

l. They are particularly user friendly for child, aged and infirm gardeners.

The ten-tub vegetable garden described in Section 3.9 is a novel approach to raised beds and has additional advantages.

3.6 HILLSIDE TERRACES

Terraces of various sizes and heights are excellent places to grow vegetables on a sloping site. The advantage is the depth of soil behind the walls, especially if you are starting from scratch and can backfill with rich soil at least for the top 40 centimetres. If you inherit terraces, they may have been used for vegetables until recently and therefore have a reasonable depth of good soil that can be easily enriched. On the other hand they may be planted with dead or dying vines or almond trees. The best thing in these circumstances is to remove the top 30 to 40 centimetres of the existing soil and replace it with a reasonable top soil then immediately enrich it with compost and manures. The initial enrichment of soils is covered in Section 4.3.

If building your own terrace walls, solid rather than dry stone walls are preferable to prevent water loss, but do include drainage tubes through the walls to run off excess water after heavy rains. If you inherit dry stone walls and water runs through them when you water, it would be worth pointing the front face.

How you use the top of the terrace for growing vegetables will depend on the distance between terrace walls. The steeper the slope the nearer and the shallower vice versa.

The possibilities include:

a. If the wall is only a metre high, work the first metre of soil as a raised bed by standing in front of the wall.

b. If the wall is higher, all the soil will need to be worked as either a vegetable plot or as two or more strip beds. One at the top of the wall and one or more further back. The advantage of the latter is that you won't need to walk on the soil you are cultivating.

c. If the wall is only a metre high and the distance between successive terraces greater than two metres, a combination of a and b could be worked.

If the terrace walls are only a metre high, the fronts can be made attractive by trailing tomatoes, cucumbers, gourds, capers or nasturtiums. The fronts of south-facing taller terrace walls can be excellent places to grow tomatoes, peppers and aubergines. The reflected heat from the walls will help them ripen earlier. A lean-to plastic greenhouse against a terrace wall would allow the growing of earlier and later crops than in the open air.

If you have a very rocky slope, a practical way of preparing to grow vegetables is to build a succession of shallow terraces — say 30-40cm deep — with a soil width of only 40-70cm before the next terrace wall. You could irrigate these strip terraces when it rains by channelling rain water from terrace to terrace down the slope.

3.7 STRIP BEDS IN ORCHARDS AND ELSEWHERE

Strip beds are, as the name implies, long areas of soil one or one-and-a-half metres wide. They are a good option midway between raised beds and a traditional square or oblong vegetable plot and are particularly useful for growing vegetables between rows of fruit trees.

The advantages are that:

- You can cultivate them without walking on the soil.
- You can rotavate them with a small rotavator in two or three runs.
- The long run can be split into a number of lengths dedicated to the different classes of vegetables and thus allowing for a crop rotation system. See Section 5.7.
- You can run three or four straight runs of drip or porous irrigation tubing down the entire length of the beds.
- Strip beds can be located anywhere in a large garden and between the rows of fruit trees in an orchard, especially when they are young. Fruit trees are normally planted with five or six metres between each. It will be many years, if ever, before their roots, which tend to go out as far as the drip line below the outer leave, interfere with you growing vegetables down the centre of the rows and vice versa.
- They can be run along the boundary fences/walls of small gardens.
- If you have the space, they are easy to expand to any length.

Equally it is easy to stop using the ends temporarily or permanently without interfering with cultivation of the remaining areas.

- A traditional vegetable plot can be worked as a series of parallel strips with permanent walking strips between.

The table below indicates the total area required for 120 square metres of strip bed compared with identical growing areas using raised beds or a traditional vegetable plot.

The area within an orchard would not be used for anything else if you do not grow vegetables or soft fruits so you do not need to allow for the walking areas on either side.

COMPARISONS BETWEEN STRIP BEDS, RAISED BEDS AND TRADITIONAL VEGETABLE PLOTS

TYPE	Total square metres required for a growing area of 100 square metres		
	Growing area	**Paths**	**Total area**
Strip bed 1m-wide in non-orchard area			
a. a single bed	120	160 a metre wide	280
b. four parallel beds	120	150 a metre wide	270
...within orchard			
a. a single bed	120	0	120
b. four parallel beds	120	0	120
Raised beds			
a.two 150-cm-wide beds	120	120 a metre wide	240
b.one 150-cm-wide centre bed and two 75-cm-wide	120	80 a metre wide	200
Vegetable plot 12x10 or 15x8m	120	20 treading area	140

3.8 FITTING VEGETABLES INTO A COTTAGE-STYLE GARDEN

A cottage-style garden implies a wide range of plants intermixed in an informal, perhaps semi-wild, manner like a jigsaw puzzle with little geometric form. They are most commonly seen in Spain in rural areas of Galicia, the north coast provinces and Pyrenean and other mountain villages.

There are several ways of incorporating vegetables and associated herbs into such a garden, including the following:

a. Vegetable plants co-planted within a mixed perennial shrub bed.

b. A small plot or several mini patches surrounded by or set in flower beds.

c. Vegetables and small fruit trees in containers spread around and integrated with other plants. Containers could be partially sunk into the ground to reduce water drainage losses.

d. A spiral snail bed (Section 2.2) or a cartwheel vegetable/herb bed as a centre piece, perhaps with a central water feature. This could be a fun way of stimulating children to be involved.

All sorts of vegetables can be incorporated into cottage-type gardens.

• Tomatoes and mixed-colour peppers for height and their coloured fruits.

• Low-growing, multicoloured oak leaf lettuces , attractive beetroot leaves or chard lining paths where they add colour and are convenient to harvest.

• Tall sunflower-headed Jerusalem artichokes at the back of a bed where they can be left undisturbed except for digging up tubers to cook each autumn when their flowers and leaves have died back.

• Cucumbers, gherkins or squashes cascading down a bank or disguising an eyesore.

• Herbs will look natural and be a normal part of the plantings in any case. They can be intermingled or placed in pots at strategic crossings of paths or around informal terraces. Rockeries planted largely with herbs or a dedicated herb garden are often incorporated into cottage-style gardens.

• Fruit bushes and trees selected from Section Five could also add character to the garden.

The only constraints are the depth and quality of your soil and your imagination.

3.9 A TEN-TUB VEGETABLE GARDEN — THE WAY OF THE FUTURE

The most productive and aesthetic small-scale method of growing vegetables in containers is what we term the "ten-tub vegetable garden" employing the large tree tubs used by garden centres. These can be purchased from horticultural suppliers. It is a very viable alternative to using traditional raised beds. We have been experimenting with this novel method for some time and it is the way we will go when we are too old to work our current 800-square-metre huerto or we lose it to building development, as happened a few years ago to our previous 400-square-metre plot.

The photograph shows the tub illustrated in Section 2.6 multiplied by three and planted with some summer crops. Later an umbrella was used to shade salad crops from the midday sun to retain moisture, slow their maturity and their going to seed. The three tubs are on a terrace but could equally be in any convenient spot in the garden.

We have found that all types of vegetables grow well in the deep, friable compost mix used to fill the tubs so it would be feasible to expand the three into a ten-tub vegetable garden, as illustrated in the sketch layout. The layout incorporates a raised water tank for gravity irrigation as an alternative to a piped supply and a greenhouse for raising plantlets.

The ten-tub concept

Three productive tubs

The most convenient sizes of tubs to use include the following.

Diameter cms	Height cms	Capacity litres
80	62	240
96	73	350
122	82	750

These tubs are a good height for working and can be worked from one side, which would be essential on a penthouse terrace. Within the garden a ten-tub unit could be surrounded by brushwood panels or a line of cordon or espalier fruit trees for a combined vegetable and fruit garden.

The space required is indicated below allowing for a one-metre pathway between the two rows of tubs. The percentage of space available for growing vegetables is very similar to that of raised beds. The space available on a vegetable plot — allowing for narrow walking spaces between rows or blocks of crops, a one-metre-wide path on one side and a couple of barrels of water for top watering — would be around 65 per cent.

Diameter cms	Space required in sqm		Growing area in sqm.	% space for growing vegetables	
	With water tank	Without water tank		With water tank	Without water tank
80	12.48	10.40	5.02	80	80
120	24.48	20.40	11.3	120	120

Since there are 10 tubs, each can be allocated to a different type of plants. One possibility is illustrated below. The following year you could rotate the root, fruit, leaf and flower vegetables — see Section 5.7.

Tub No	Crops autum/winter	Crops spring/summer
1	Salad leaf crops/radishes	Salad leaf crops/radishes
2	Vegetable leaf crops	Vegetable leaf crops
3	Onions/garlic/leeks	Onions/garlic/leeks
4	Carrots/onions/beetroot	Carrots/parsnips/onions
5	Broad beans and cascading	Peppers & aubergines or tomatoes
6	Sprouting broccoli /calabrese	Dwarf French beans & cascading courgettes and cucumbers
7	Potatoes (autumn and spring) and Jerusalem artichokes (spring to autumn)	
8	Permanent edible herb bed	
9	Permanent asparagus bed with co-planted tomato plants when the weather allows	
10	Permanent Alpìne strawberry/raspberry bed	

Yes, we would include a tub of soft fruit such as Alpine strawberries and raspberries. These both yield fruit on our allotment for six months a year. One vital additional crop for us would be the valuable herb comfrey (see Section 5.3) which we would grow under and around the raised water tank. If you are a lover of watercress, one of the tubs could be lined with pond plastic and filled with water. Fresh water would need to run through daily but the overflow could be collected in a tank alongside and used for watering the other tubs using a small solar-powered pump.

To cope with hot summer suns, a woven-plastic shade could be run on wires above the tubs. During the winter/early spring it would be easy to cover some of the tubs with clear plastic sheeting stretched over wire hoops to protect emerging seedlings and young plants.

As with all small growing areas, a ten-tub vegetable garden would be most productive if plantlets were used where possible rather than raising everything from seed in the tubs. In the sketch a small greenhouse is shown alongside the water tank for the raising of seasonal plantlets.

Naturally 10 tubs is not the limit. You could add as many as you like for growing additional vegetables including squash and even a giant pumpkin, and a child could be allocated one as their very own garden.

3.10 THE SUCCESS FACTOR – YOUR NANO CLIMATES

There are three levels of climate that will affect the success of your vegetable growing wherever you are situated and whatever style of vegetable growing you decide on. Namely the macro, micro and nano climates.

As illustrated in the table, the first you can do nothing about except by moving house, the second you can modify to a degree and the third, the nano climate is entirely in your hands. How far you modify it will determine how successful you will be. The important thing is to realise that the macro and micro climates are above ground while the nano climate is both above and below ground.

The starting point for achieving an optimum nano climate for your vegetables is to prepare the soil before you start — both in a general way (section 4.3) and in a specific way for each group of vegetables (sections 4.5 to 4.8). Other sections of Part Four deal with a wide range of issues generally applicable whichever way you intend to grow vegetables.

THREE DIMENSIONS OF CLIMATE THAT WILL AFFECT VEGETABLE GROWTH

Macro climate: the general pattern of annual and seasonal hours sunshine, temperatures, wind, humidity, rain, frost, hail and snow in your area.
Micro climate: the extent, pattern and balance of sunshine, shade, protection from hot and cold drying winds, and beneficial wildlife achieved as a result of the design and construction of your garden and the location of your vegetable plot within the overall plan.
Nano climate: very localised conditions, above and below ground, relating to and affecting groups of vegetable plants and individual plants whether in a plot or pots etc.
The third is the most important and the one most easily improved by yourself.

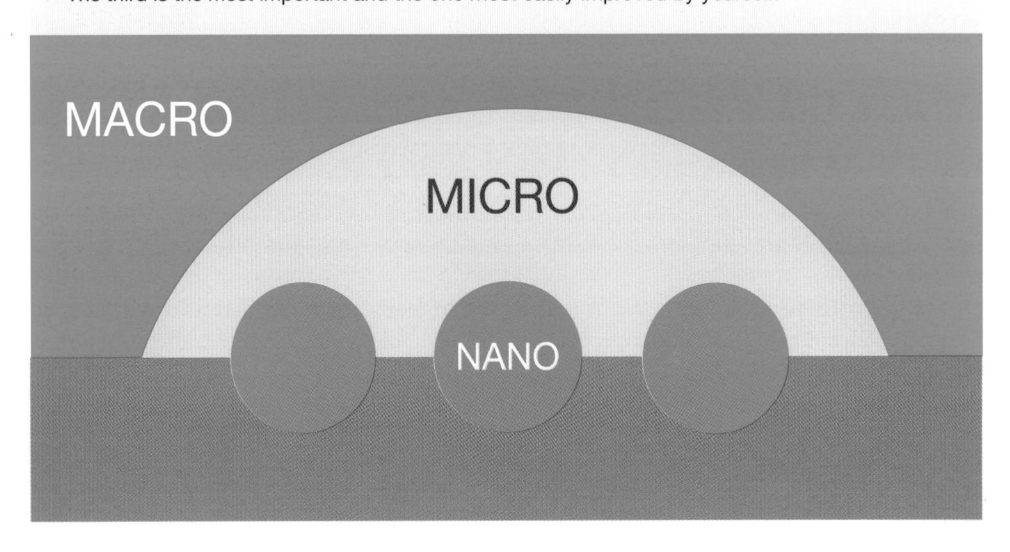

CHARACTERISTICS OF:

POOR NANO CLIMATE

ABOVE GROUND

1. No beneficial insects
2. Constant insecticide/fungicide mist
3. Watering of leaves causing fungal attacks
4. No shade or shelter from hot/cold winds
5. Hard solid soil surface

BELOW GROUND

1. Lacks natural nutrients
2. Compacted solid mass
3. No worms
4. Sterile and with very few microbes, mostly bad
5. Variable moisture, either dry or waterlogged
6. Roots force-fed with fast chemical fertilisers

GOOD NANO CLIMATE

ABOVE GROUND

1. Beneficial insects, animals and birds
2. Symbiotic companion plantings
3. Surface watering except for rain
4. Wind breaks and natural shading
5. Regularly loosened surface soil

BELOW GROUND

1. Natural nutrients available in the soil
2. Open crumbly aerated soil structure
3. Large worm population
4. Full of beneficial microbes
5. Constant moisture, never waterlogged
6. Roots take what they want from the soil

3.11 WHICH IS FOR YOU AND YOUR FAMILY?

You have now read about all the options, so which is best for you? To help you make that decision, the table below summarises which are in our view most appropriate for a number of typical situations.

OPTIONS	**INDICATION OF OPTIONS NOST SUITABLE FOR EXPANDING OR STARTING TO GROW VEGETABLES ON A LARGER SCALE**							
	PENTHOUSE TERRACE	**APARTMENT TERRACE**	**PATIO GARDEN**	**SMALL GARDEN**	**LARGER PROPERTY**	**MOUNTAIN SIDE**	**ELDERLY PERSON**	**CHILDREN**
Collections of containers	*	*	*	*	*	*	*	
Traditional vegetable plot				*	*			*(1)
Larger-scale plot				Could Rent	*	Could Rent		
Raised beds	*	*	*	*	*	*	*	*
Hillside terraces				*	*	*		
Strip beds in orchards					*			*(1)
Cottage-style garden				*	*			*(1)
Ten-tub vegetable garden	*	Five-tub possible	Five-tub possible	*	*	*	*	*(1)

Note: (1) A small area within.

Containers, raised beds and ten-tub gardens require less time to tend than the other options using the natural or imported soil. The other options can be expanded more easily if you have a villa garden or finca.

For those impaired, aged and infirm, raised beds and tub beds are the easiest to work as they can be adjusted to the most convenient working height. The next best are large containers.

For children, the most convenient are: a sand pit converted into a low raised bed, a small plot in the corner of your larger vegetable plot, strip beds, or a cartwheel design within a cottage garden for fun.

Having decided which way to go, the next question is: what to grow and how to do it? All the issues involved are covered in Part Four.

PART FOUR

HOW TO GROW HEALTHY WHOLESOME VEGETABLES

Provides practical guidelines and tips for growing more than one hundred vegetables from seeds and plantlets.

4.1 THE CHALLENGE

There are six related challenges to growing your vegetables in Spain:

- Growing sufficient to satisfy your total needs for 365 days a year, or at least sufficient of your favourite seasonal vegetables.
- Growing a greater diversity than traditionally grown here.
- Harnessing the best of the Spanish weather and avoiding damage from the worst.
- Improving your soils and growing your vegetables naturally, ecologically and organically as defined below.
- Making the most productive use of the area of good soil you have available whether in containers, raised beds, within flower beds or as a traditional vegetable plot of any size.
- Economising on the use of scarce expensive water.

Growing naturally means growing vegetables that are of a normal size, with good texture packed with natural flavours, aromas, vitamins and minerals. Grown at a natural rate in enriched soil with the minimum need for extra feeding, rather than forced, over-watered and over-fed giants often with little taste and a watery texture.

Growing ecologically means protecting or in most cases re-establishing the natural mix and balance of beneficial microbes, insects, animals and birds in, on and around the earth in which you grow your vegetables and modifying the way you work your soil so that the need for fertilisers, insecticides and fungicides is minimised and the need for herbicides avoided.

Growing organically means that when fertilisers, insecticides and fungicides are necessary that only ones based on natural plants, animal manures and minerals are used rather than synthetic inorganic chemical products.

Compared to five years ago there are many natural and non-chemical alternatives available to meet any problem. We strongly recommend using them.

Provided you are not in a heavy frost pocket or above the regular snow line, we suggest you start your vegetable-growing in the autumn rather than the spring, for three reasons:

- You will gain your first experience of growing vegetables in Spain in cooler weather with less need for constant watering than spring/summer vegetable-growing requires.
- Worms will be more active in the cooler, damper, higher levels of soil than during hot summer days. This will help improve your soil, as discussed in the next section.
- You can start a compost heap ready to use in the spring when planting fruit vegetables.

4.2 THE ESSENTIAL SUCCESS FACTORS

Growing vegetables can be good for one's health but it also needs to be done in a way that is enjoyable, self-sustaining, within your time and physical capabilities, and economic as well as enhancing the enjoyment of preparing and eating meals and snacks. The success factors for achieving this include the following:

a. A genuine interest in eating well.

b. The reliable availability of water for at least part of the year.

c. The choice of a scale and style of growing vegetables that is manageable by yourself, with reliable family help or the employment of a gardener.

d. Maximising the use of the soil area available by ensuring that it is always planted with an edible crop or green manure.

e. If you are short of space or want to grow early crops in the spring/summer or autumn/winter, don't sow seeds directly into your soil but purchase or grow your own plantlets in pots or trays.

f. Take advantage of the fact that Spain really has two springs, autumn and spring. Many crops can be sown before rather than after the winter and in some cases both autumn and spring sowings can be made. Some crops such as lettuces can be sown continuously. With others, such as potatoes, three crops can often be grown.

g. Select a mix of root, fruit, leaf and flower vegetables that will yield an interesting diversity season by season.

h. Before you sow or plant anything improve the soil.

i. Locate different varieties of vegetables so that any beneficial relations can be exploited and antagonistic ones avoided.

j. Use a lunar calendar to sow, plant, feed, harvest and work the soil on the most productive days.

k. If you live in a dust bowl in the summer or a frost basin in the winter, don't fight nature. Go mini during these times as explained in Part Two.

l. Do likewise if there are times of the year when you are short of water. For this reason many gardeners only grow vegetables from October to June.

j. Use ergonomic tools to reduce the strain of working the soil.

k. Evaluate your progress and aim towards growing your vegetables naturally, ecologically and organically (section 5.8).

4.3 IMPROVING THE SOIL BEFORE YOU START

A. The need

In general vegetables need a better soil than is necessary for most flowering shrubs and trees because:

a. Vegetables need to extract sufficient nutrients from the soil for them to complete their life cycle of germination, growth and, in some cases, flowering and fruiting ready for harvesting in only a few months, whereas shrubs and trees are best allowed to grow and mature slowly over a number of years.

b. To secure the necessary nourishment, the roots of young vegetables need to spread speedily and dive deep to extract nutrients and moisture from soil below the surface levels that soon dry out under the hot Spanish sun.

c. The roots need a constant reservoir of moisture around them to enable the nutrients to dissolve and be extractable.

An ideal soil for growing vegetables will therefore have the following characteristics:

- Crumbly and friable.
- High in humus (decomposed vegetable matter).
- Water-retaining due to the humus content but sufficiently gritty/sandy to allow excess water to drain away.
- Structure allowing roots to spread and go down deeply and sideways to find nutrients and moisture.
- Deep enough for the roots of root crops.
- Attracts and retains earthworms that process humus, which makes the nutrients in the soil more easily accessible to the roots as well as most importantly opening up the soil to improve drainage and ensure that the soil is aerated to stop it going stale.
- Damp soil particles have sufficient bonding to prevent tall vegetable plants from toppling over with the weight of their leaves and fruit.
- Does not bake hard during the first sunny day after rain.
- Not full of rocks.
- Has been worked ecologically and organically without resorting to inorganic manufactured chemical fertilisers, pesticides, fungicides or herbicides.
- Slightly acidic.

Unfortunately such soils are not that easily found in Spanish gardens. Unless you buy loads of new topsoil, the following problems cannot be corrected: topsoil removed by builder and not replaced; very shallow soil over bedrock; planting holes require a pneumatic drill; soil full of large stones or rocks; saline soils as a result of over-use of wells or felling of forests or orchards some years before.

However, most gardeners start off with one of the following problematic soils which can be reasonably easily improved. Where not, vegetables can be grown in containers, raised beds and tubs above the ground as explained in Part Three.

CORRECTABLE SOIL PROBLEMS

1. A red or grey clay soil, heavy to work when wet and impossible to work when dry and sun-baked. But often rich in minerals not easily extractable by fast growing vegetables. Dries out quickly and roots can be squeezed/strangled by the drying compacting soil in hot weather. Moisture evaporates by capillary action when the soil is baked hard.

2. A sandy soil, light in nutrients as millions of years of rain have washed away many of the minerals to the subsoil or the water table. Drains quickly and may be acidic.

3. Good topsoil bulldozed under poor subsoil by builders.

4. Peaty acid soil low in nutrients if on mountainside with spring snow melt.

5. Barren soil due to over-use or use of chemical fertilisers with no addition of organic matter for years.

6. Poor soil full of builder's rubble.

7. A naturally fertile soil full of stones and or rocks.

B. How can correctable soils be improved?

The following process needs to be followed.

a. If you have types listed as 6 and 7, remove all the offending large rocks and stones down to 30 to 40 centimetres deep. Be prepared for a hard slog — the stone walls and terrace walls you see in much of the countryside are the result of similar labour. Consider raised beds or tubs before you commit yourself to a traditional vegetable plot.

b. Soils of types 1 to 6 will need the working-in of considerable quantities of natural organic soil-improver, preferably before you grow any vegetables (see section C below). But you could start by improving part of the land earmarked for vegetables and then expand gradually as you have sufficient soil improvement material and time available.

C. What nutrients do vegetables require?

The following natural nutrients are required by vegetables to grow healthily. Some types of vegetable require more of some main nutrients than others, as will be explained in Sections 4.5 to 4.8.

From the air through the leaves

• Carbon dioxide which is taken in through the leaves at night to create chlorophyll essential to cell structures and the green colouration of vegetables.

- Moisture taken in from the air which gives cell stability together with water from the soil.
- Nitrogen through the leaves should you spray with a nitrogen-rich foliar feed.

From the soil through the roots

Apart from moisture which with micro-organisms creates rigidity and strength in stems, branches and leaves, a number of minerals and trace elements are essential for plant health and vitality.

• Nitrogen (N) which stimulates the development of stems and leaves and their green colouration.

• Phosphorus (P) in the form of phosphates which stimulate the development of strong root structures, early growth and the steady formation of mature plants.

• Potassium (K), often called potash, essential for developing resistance to drought and disease and developing flower buds, flowers, seed heads and fruits. It is essential in achieving the crispness, colour and flavour of vegetables.

• Magnesium and manganese, both of which help prevent the yellowing of leaves.

• Calcium for cell growth and resistance to disease.

• Sulphur for general plant health and resistance to fungi. Can also raise soil acidity which makes it easier for roots to extract trace minerals from the soil.

• Iron which prevents the bleaching of leaves.

• Zinc which prevents leaves from developing yellow spots.

• Smaller quantities of boron, copper and molybdenum are also required. They contribute to cell structures and natural disease control.

D. What can be used to improve your soil?

For home-grown vegetables the best way is to add organic matter in the form of composted green plant waste and animal manures. The following are the most frequently available and cost-effective.

Purchasable natural organic soil improvers	Relative convenience	Relative cost	Need to process before using	Relative nutrient content	Relative humus content
1. A load or bags of animal manure from a local stable or farm					
a. horses and donkeys	M	L	H*	M	H
b. sheep and goats	M	L	H*	H	H
2. A load or bags of poultry manure from a local chicken house	M	L	H*	H	M/H
3. Plastic sacks of commercially prepared bags of dried/partially dried manures/composts	H	M	L	H	H
4. Plastic sacks of worm compost	H	H	L	H	M
5. Sacks of guano, e.g. Trabe Guanaforte (www,trabe.net)	H	M	L	H	H
6. Sacks of spent mushroom compost	H	M	L	L	H
7. Ecopark compost from green waste	M	L	L	L/M	H
7. Ecopark compost as above plus with added composted seaweed	M	L	L	M	H
8. Sacks of proprietary organic fibrous compost with added organic manures	H	M/H	L	M	H

Home producible or collectable natural organic soil improvers	Relative convenience	Relative cost	Need to process before using	Relative nutrient content	Relative humus content
9. Home produced manures					
a. horses, donkeys, mules	H	L	H*	M/H*	H
b. sheep & goats	H	L	H*	H	M
c. rabbits & guinea pigs	H	L	M*	M	M/H
d. chickens & turkeys	H	L	H*	H	M
10. Spent mushrooms growing sacks	H	L	L	L	H
11. Growing of greeen manures such as alfalfa & phacellia	M	M	L	M	H
12. Compost from your own compost heap	M	L	L	L	H
13. As `12´ with layers of manures	M	L	L	M/H	M/H
14. Seaweed swept onto local beaches by storms	M/L	L	M*	H	H
15. Worm compost from a home wormery	M	M/H*	L	H	M
16. Wood ash from old wood	H	L	L	M	L

Notes: H = High: M = Medium: L = Low
* Need to be composted before use or layered into a compost heap.
** Taking into account cost of unit and slow production rate.

E. How much organic matter should be added to the soil?

We suggest the following guidelines.

1. Aim towards 25 to 40 per cent added organic matter in poor soils. In practice it may take you several years to achieve this.

2. To fill moderate-sized raised beds or a ten-tub vegetable garden as described in Part Three, aim at a mix of 30/40 per cent compost to 60 per cent of a reasonable soil mix or one of the following:

Mix A: 10 per cent manures, 30 per cent Ecopark compost, 10 per cent coarse sand with 50 per cent soil.

Mix B: 10 per cent worm compost, 90 per cent compost with seaweed from Ecopark which has a visible sand content.

Mix C: 30 per cent of our own manure-enriched compost, 40 per cent Ecopark compost, 10 per cent sand, 20 per cent soil.

3. To do the same thing on a large area of raised beds, a vegetable plot or huerto would require considerable quantities of material.
The following are four more practical approaches.

a. Cover the soil with two 20-litre builder's baskets (capachos) of Ecopark compost and two builder's baskets of Ecopark compost with added seaweed plus a basket of composted animal manure/bagged manure per square metre and dig or rotavate it into the top 20 to 30 centimetres of the soil.

b. Cover the surface of the soil with two to four baskets of home-produced compost plus one of manure per square metre and dig/rotavate in.

c. As b but cover the area with a sheet of black plastic or old carpets to let worms work the humus into the soil before digging or rotavating.

d. Start off by adding four 20-litre builder's baskets of Ecopark compost per square metre of growing area and then dig/rotavate in followed by only growing a green manure on the whole area for the first four months. Then cut the crop and dig or rotavate into the soil and leave for two months before preparing to plant vegetables. Then repeat the growing of the green manure on a fifth of the soil every six months on a rotation basis. Over a number of years you would end up with an extremely good soil and could claim that you were growing biologically as some commercial growers of "naturally" produced vegetables do.

The key is to use as much organic material as you can on a poor soil. If you over-do it the first year, which is unlikely, vegetables may grow a little forced but you can correct that by not adding supplementary top-ups the following year. This is better than under-enriching and having to continually use supplementary feeds to keep vegetables growing (see Section 5.3).

Alternatively, if you believe your soil is reasonably good, reduce the above quantities by half and see how the first year goes. You can then add more the second year if necessary.

Whatever you do, some vegetables will benefit from special treatment when sown (as explained in Sections 4.5 to 4.8).

F. Other possible start-up additives

Soil's acidity affects the ability of vegetables to extract the nutrients. In general a slightly acid soil is required for vegetables. Acidity is measured on a Ph scale from 1 to 14. The highest level of acidity is a measure of 1 and the highest level of alkalinity is a measure of 14, while 7 is regarded as neutral. The Ph scale is logarithmic. A Ph value of 5 is 10 times the acidity of 6 and likewise a value of 4 is 10 times the acidity level of 5.

Typical preferred Ph levels are:

7.0 to 6.5: asparagus, beans, lettuces, onions and spinach.

7.0 to 6.0: broad beans, dwarf and climbing beans, broccoli, sweet corn, parsnips, squash, and turnips.

6.5 to 5.5: courgettes, potatoes, and tomatoes. Raspberries, strawberries and red currants also like an acid soil.

6.0 to 5.5: potatoes. They can in fact grow well at any of the other acidity levels, but scab disease is normally less of a problem at higher acidity levels.

The best way to test your soil is to use a Ph meter which has a stem that you can stick in the ground or measure an emulsion of soil stirred up in water. In the latter case also check the Ph of the water alone as, if not 7, this could distort your soil acidity reading. A strip of litmus paper which comes with a simple chart or a more complex soil testing kit can also be used.

If you need to adjust your Ph levels, composts and manures are normally slightly acid so the additions discussed in previous section will have helped. If soil tests indicate that the soil acidity is still low, sulphur powder can be shaken on the soil and either mixed in or allowed to be washed into the soil by rain.

The Ph value of soil can be best lowered naturally (i.e. made more acid) by using stored rain water. Also bagged worm compost reduces acidity levels. The acidity of soils and irrigation water is discussed in section 4.18.

G. Increasing the worm population

The final important ingredient in a good soil for growing vegetables is a large and active worm population.

This is important for three reasons:

- Worms feed on the humus in the soil and therefore their excreta is very rich in nutrients in a form easily accessible to the roots of vegetable plants.
- When soils are moist they will work the upper layers of the soil taking down any new surface humus.
- The worm passage ways help lighten the soil and allow air in to stop the soil becoming stale or stagnant.

Unfortunately, the soil in many gardens starts off with few worms so it is important to increase the population as soon as possible.

There are three practical things you can do. Firstly, well-rotted farmyard manure is likely to have a good worm population. Secondly, the humus you have added to your soil will provide them with ample food and an ideal nano climate in which to breed. Thirdly, once you start a compost heap (Section 5.5) worms will normally be attracted to the base of the heap and then work their way up layer by layer, breeding on the way.

When you empty your fully composted heaps, always share any resident worm population between the compost that you take out to work into the soil and the next batch of compost. We always recycle several buckets of the compost with the highest concentration of worms into the base of the next batch of vegetable waste to be composted. Provided you keep the growing compost heap damp, they won't disappear.

To protect the valuable population of worms in the soil, do not burn bonfires on your vegetable-growing area and don't treat the soil with chemicals to kill off eel worms or cut worms. The chemicals used can be very lethal for earth worms as well.

4.4 WHAT CAN BE GROWN, WHERE, WHEN AND HOW?

If you are in an ideal microclimate along the Mediterranean coast or connected inland valleys and have an adequate supply of water all year around, the answer is: almost anything. In essence you will be able to harvest a good range of vegetables every day of the year.

However, if you live in a summer dust bowl with a limited supply of water, it would be wise only to grow your vegetables on a major scale during the cooler months of the autumn, winter and spring. As explained in the next sections, there are plenty of vegetables that can be grown at those times. Likewise, if you are in a heavy winter frost pocket or above the snow line, what you grow in the winter will be restricted.

In our valley there are few winter restrictions on the south-facing slopes which have sun all day and just the occasional frost, but it is very difficult to grow winter vegetables on the north-facing slope that has weeks of frost and few hours of sun.

When one can start to sow and plant vegetables in the autumn varies little region to region. The only constraints will be how late temperatures drop below 30 degrees, how early the autumn rains come and the probability of frosts. We know of gardeners who wait patiently, very patiently at times, for the autumn rains to fill their well or local supply reservoir sufficiently to be able to irrigate late tomatoes and peppers in a south-facing greenhouse.

However there are major variations in sowing and planting out times in the late winter and early spring related to the likelihood of late frost.

The main differences are:

a. Sowings and plantings on the coastal plain are likely to be two weeks ahead of those on vegetables plots 200 metres up and possibly a month ahead of those at 400 metres.

b. Sowings on the coastal plain will be similarly two to four weeks ahead of inland areas along a river valley that has late frosts. For instance, sowings of onions are often two weeks later in the central areas of the Guadalquivir valley in Andulusia than in the huertos surrounding Valencia and those in the Ebro valley in Catalonia a week or two behind the Guadalquivir.

c. You might plant out tomatoes in March on the coast but have to wait until June in a high Pyrenean village.

d. If your vegetable plot is completely sheltered from cold winds by a mountainside, valley walls, trees and fences, your soil will warm up a week or so earlier than a totally exposed plot a hundred metres away.

e. If you allow your vegetables to grow naturally during the winter months, they are likely to survive extraordinary frosts better than larger faster-growing plants forced by extra watering and feeding. By doing this we survived the cold spell during the winter of 2004/5 rather better than some nearby Spanish neighbours.

f. On the other hand you will be able to plant tomatoes and peppers as well as potatoes in November on the southern coast of

Grand Canary and in frost-free areas of the Costa del Sol and Costa Tropical. Your March vegetable garden will look like a July garden in Valencia. If you have the water, further crops can be planted in the spring for the summer.

So, before you make your first late winter/early spring plantings, watch out for the first plantlets on sale, the first plantings by local commercial growers under plastic and in the open air, when commercial growers open up the tunnel cloches over early plantings and check with a few expatriate and Spanish neighbours.

Don't worry if you are a week late with plantings either in the spring or autumn. They will soon catch up in a warm spell.

To summarise: if you have near-ideal conditions, a wide range of vegetables can be grown 12 months of the year. If not, they can still be grown for nine months of the year in the hottest areas and for seven months in villages above the regular snowline.

The tables presented in Sections 4.5 to 4.8 assume that you are in situations where it is possible to grow vegetables throughout the year. They provide practical guidelines for growing a wide range of vegetables. In total 90 vegetables are included in the tables. For convenience they are grouped as follows: Section 4.5 root vegetables; 4.6 fruit vegetables; 4.7 leaf vegetables and herbs and 4.8 flower vegetables and companion plants. This grouping also makes it easier to relate them to the lunar calendar (Section 4.15), which can help improve the productivity of your sowings and to a crop rotation plan (Section 5.6), that can help you avoid build-ups of soil-borne plant pests and diseases.

Each of the four sections includes concise basic guidelines and special tips that are presented as a combination of tables and notes.

The tables indicate what can be grown (essentially what we have grown to date), whether to grow for salads or vegetable dishes, whether best grown from seed or first as plantlets, when best to sow and/or plant out, typical harvesting times, special soil and extra feed needs, moisture needs for healthy growth and the common pests, diseases and other problems that each vegetable might be vulnerable to.

The tips that follow for each vegetable are designed to help you decide which varieties of each vegetable to grow and provide you with extra information not included in the tables that will help you grow good vegetables here in Spain. The most important issues are also expanded on in a general way in the sections that follow, i.e. Sections 4.9 etc.

These practical guidelines focus on helping you grow your vegetables at a natural pace and to a natural size so that they will be:

a. At their best when you harvest and eat them.

b. Less likely to attract pests and disease while growing and, if they do, will be sufficiently healthy and strong to cope with them with minimum treatment.

c. Slower to go to seed in the hottest weather.

d. Less likely to suffer seriously from winter frosts.

e. In less need of watering and extra feeding than if you tried to grow large water-filled vegetables of an unnatural size.

We have grown some very large specimens but they were the result of starting with good seeds which included by luck a few "super seeds", plus the right soil conditions and worked depth, the perfect climatic conditions (not too much over 30 degrees and no cold shocks), beneficial rainfall during their growth and careful weeding. We are still searching for a 'super seed" to grow a 100-kilo pumpkin for fun. The heaviest so far weighed 60 kilos.

The guidelines in Sections 4.5 to 4.8 recognise that we can do nothing to change the

macro climate of the area we live in and only go so far to achieve a more benign garden micro climate in which strategically placed trees, walls and fences protect the vegetable plot from the worst of the hot summer and freezing winter gales. But what we can do is to create an optimum nano climate for each row or block of plants according to the needs of the particular type of vegetable being grown.

The tables included in Sections 4.5. to 4.8 refer to winter, spring, summer and autumn. We regard these as:

December/January/February: winter.
March/April/May: spring.
June/July/August: summer.
September/October/November: autumn.

Where essential, we have also referred to early or late spring, March being early and May being late.

Read through the guideline sections and you will be in a position to decide what you will grow yourself, as discussed in Section 4.9. Sections 4.5 to 4.8 and all the later sections will guide you step by step through their sowing and growing directly from seed in pots, tubs, raised beds or vegetable plots or by first growing plantlets.

Section 5.8 provides a practical basis for evaluating your progress. We wish you luck.

4.5 PRACTICAL TIPS FOR GROWING ROOT CROPS

VEGETABLES **English** *Spanish*	**For salads (S) veget (V)**	**Grown from S* SD** ST P/Rh/Tu***	**When - Autumn Winter Spring Summer A/W/Sp/S**	**Sow/plant in rows (R) blocks (B)**
ONION FAMILY				
Chives *Cebollinos*	S/V	SD P	Sp Sp	R/B R/B
Garlic *Ajos*	S/V	Cloves SD	LA/EW	R/B
Onions *(Cebollas)* **a.**non-storing (grown over winter) **b.** storing (grown during spring summer)	 S/V S/V	 S* ST/P SD* ST/P	 LS/EA LA/EW LW/ESp LSp/ES	 R/B R/B R/B R/B
Onions - multiplier shallot *(Cebollas de multiplicadora/ Chalotes*	S/V	ST	LW/ESp	R/B
Spring onions/scallions *Cebolletas*	S/V	SD	LW/ESp	R/B
OTHERS				
Beetroots *Remolacha*	S/V	SD** P	EA/LW ESp A/Sp	R/B
Carrots *Zanahorias*	S/V	SD*	LS/A/LW/ LW/Sp	R/B
Celeriac *Apio/nabo*	V	SD* P	LS/EA/ LW/ES A/Sp	RB

Typical harvest times Autumn Winter Spring Summer A/W/Sp. S	**Soil needs (1-8) & C**	**Extra feed needs N P K C M**	**Moisture needs High (H) Medium (M) Low (L)**	**Common pests and diseases (See Section 5.7) and other problems**
Sp to EW	5/6	-	M	-
Sp/ES	5/6	Dilute liquid seaweed	L	Onion fly Fungal disease
Sp/ES	5/6	-	M See below	As above
A	5/6	-		
ES	5/6	-	M	As above
Sp/ES	5/6	-	M	As above
W+S	2	Dilute liquid seaweed	M	Avoid sporadic watering - can cause splitting and hard cores
All year	5	-	W	Carrot fly. Avoid sporadic watering - can cause forking roots & hard cores
S/A	2	-	H	-

VEGETABLES **English** *Spanish*	**For salads (S) veget (V)**	**Grown from S* SD** ST P/Rh/Tu***	**When - Autumn Winter Spring Summer A/W/Sp/S**	**Sow/plant in rows (R) blocks (B)**
OTHERS				
Ginger *Jenjibre*	S/V	Rh*	Sp	-
Jerusalem artichokes *Tupinambos*	S/V	Tu	LW/ESp	R
Parsnips *Chirivias*	V	SD**	LS/A + LW/Sp	R/B
Peanuts *Cacahuetes*	Tapa	SD (nuts)	Lsp	R
Potatoes *Patatas*	V	Tu	LS Sp	R
Radishes *Rábanos/rabanitos*	S/V	SD	LW/Sp + LS/A	R/B
Sweet potatoes *Boniatos*	V	Tu	LW/Sp	R
Turnip *Nabo*	V	SD*	Sp/ES + LS/EA	R
Tiger nuts *Horchata*	V	SD	Sp	R
Tumeric	V	Tu*	W/Sp	B

Notes:

A. - guide to abbreviations

ESp = Early spring.

LSp = Late spring.

S = Seeds sown in containers - * plantlets planted out later.

SD = Seeds sown directly in ground *thinned out - ** thinnings can be transplanted.

ST = Grow from sets.

P/Rh/Tu = Plantlets, rhizomes, tubers planted directly in ground -* planted in containers.

Typical harvest times Autumn Winter Spring Summer A/W/Sp. S	Soil needs (1-8) & C	Extra feed needs N P K C M	Moisture needs High (H) Medium (M) Low (L)	Common pests and diseases (See Section 5.7) and other problems
W	2	-	M	Rotting off - do not over water Dislikes full sun - grows well in semi shade under trees
A	2	-	L	Rotting off - do not over water
All year	5	-	M	Avoid sporadic watering - can cause forking roots and hard cores
LS/EA	2	P	M	Wireworm
W S/A	2 + 6	-	M	Scab/mildew/Colorado beetle/ wireworm and eelworm. Rotting off - do not overwater
LW/Sp + A/EW	5	-	M	Avoid sporadic watering - can cause forking roots and hard cores
LS/A	2 + 6	-	H	Rotting off - do not overwater
S/A + W	5	-	L	If soil is acid feed with liquid seaweed
A	2	P	M	Wireworm
S/A	2	-	M	-

N = High in nitrogen feed.
K = High in phosphorus/phosphate feed.
P = High in potassium/potash feed.
C = High in calcium (lime) feed.
M = Mulch with comfrey leaves.

B. Soil Needs

1. Soil enriched with plenty of manure/compost. Will tolerate partially decomposed/ fresh manure.
2. As above but all must be fully decomposed.
3. Trenches dug and filled with well-rotted manure/compost and capped with soil a month before sowing.
4. Large holes dug and filled with well-rotted/manure/compost during the previous winter.
5. Grows best in soil well-enriched for preceding crops with no extra compost/manure added. Detests fresh compost.
6. A little wood ash added to the soil before planting.
7. Grows best in soil enriched in nitrogen by previous pea and bean crops.
8. As soil 2 with added grit or coarse sand.

C. If you have not enriched your soil as in Section 4.3. you will need to resort to feeding all root crops with a granular or liquid general fertiliser high in phosphorus/phosphate weekly from the day you plant to the day you harvest. In all cases we recommend you use a natural ecological/organic food rather than manufactured chemicals.

OTHER TIPS

Chives

- Best planted on ridges as they don't like wet soil.
- They die back over winter so, once they start to grow again in the spring, harvest continuously to stop flowers forming. Once flowering the flowers are tasty but their stalks are hard and inedible. Cut back hard to stimulate new growth.
- Excess crops can be chopped up and stored in an airtight jar with crushed garlic and olive oil. Makes a good addition to salads.

Garlic

- Varieties: buy bulbs to plant from your local agricultural cooperative, outdoor market or even the supermarket. The best for storing are the pink-skinned varieties.
- By early spring you will be able to harvest young garlic and use in salads like spring onions.
- In early summer, once the leaves have died back and the cloves have formed, dig up and dry in the sun on trays.
- Organically grown garlic, grown at a natural rate, is not normally as large as commercially grown garlic but it is very full of oil and tasty. When completely dry, store in a dry cool place on trays or tie up in plaits, bunches or hang in mesh bags.

Onions

- Varieties: two crops are normally grown in Spain. The first is of non-storing varieties planted from plantlets in late autumn to early winter and harvested from early spring to early summer. The second consists of main crop varieties planted from plantlets and sets in late spring and early summer and harvested for storing from late summer onwards. You can harvest the non-storing varieties at whatever stage you like. We normally harvest some young to eat in salads so that we do not have a glut of mature poor-storing onions. Once the weather heats up they go to seed very fast. Any excess crops will store for a short time if you store them on trays in a cool place. Main crop varieties have normal watering needs until the leaves start to die back and the bulbs are swelling when watering should be discontinued until they are harvested. As soon as the leaves have died back, dig up and put on trays in a well-ventilated, dry, shady place for several weeks or until completely dry. Store on trays or hung up in mesh bags or plaited in a dry place.

  Harvest all root crops on a root day according to the lunar calendar for better storage.

Other varieties – small cocktail, spring onions/scallions, pickling onions, medium/large sized reds, whites, browns. Seeds for very large exhibition types can also be purchased by mail order.

Beetroots

- Varieties: globe and long-rooted, miniature and standard, red, orange, and yellow-skinned. The dark red varieties tend to be the tastiest.
- Thin out young plants for salads leaving the remainder to mature for the main harvest. Unless below zero for a long period can be left in ground over winter.

Carrots

- Varieties – baby round, cylindrical, long tapered, bright orange, red and yellow. Reliable varieties are Chantenay red-cored and Nantes. We also search through UK catalogues for the brightest orange and red varieties which are the highest in carotene.
- Emergent carrot seedlings are very fine and unfortunately are loved by slugs and snails. So ensure that you put down traps as soon as you sow the seeds.
- Thin out continuously and use young roots for salads.
- Carrots can be harvested throughout the year but their growth will slow down during the colder winter months. We don't find it necessary to dig them and store them.

Root ginger

- Plant a piece of root/rhizome with two sprouting nodes.
- Harvest when leaves die back in the autumn.
- Keep some rhizomes in dry compost in a dark cellar to replant the following spring.
- To store: cut into 4cm pieces, put into freezer bags and freeze. You can then use it by grating what you need when it is still frozen and putting it back once more in the freezer, or alternatively grate the freshly harvested rhizomes, put in small jars and cover with olive oil.

Jerusalem artichokes

- Harvest in the autumn when leaves die back. Keep some tubers in dry compost in a dark cellar to replant the following spring.

Parsnips

- Parsnips can be difficult to germinate. Make sure your seed is very fresh, water seed bed well before planting and don't allow to dry out.
- Harvest as you need them from late summer to early winter. Can overwinter in the ground.

Peanuts

- If you have wild boar in your area, beware. They can demolish your peanut crop fast. A simple solution is to fill small cotton bags with human hair and tie them strategically around your plot.
- Harvest in autumn when the leaves start to die back. Wash off the soil and lay out to dry for several days in the sun. Once dry, store in airtight containers. Shell them and eat them raw or roast in a little salt.

Potatoes

- The number of varieties in Spain is limited. The best you will find is probably a national white, and regional reds, occasionally a flowery Canary Island variety and unusual white/black French varieties. The latter we look for in specialist greengrocers.
- If there is any likelihood of frost after you have planted in late autumn for your Christmas harvest or in early spring, make sure you earth up any early growth and if necessary cover with a layer of straw or fleece.
- In early summer harvest as tasty new potatoes after flowers have formed or dig up in late

summer when the leaves have died off. Those planted for a winter crop can be harvested before Christmas.

- Store mature crops in trays in a cool dry cellar.

Radishes

- Many varieties to choose from. To prevent them from going to seed in the hot summer weather it helps to give them some shading.

Sweet potatoes

- To grow – place a tuber (which you can buy from your local supermarket) in a deep seed tray and cover with damp mature compost. When the young shoots have grown to 15cm-long, cut off with a piece of the tuber attached about the size of a euro. Plant these shoots in pots and, when good roots have formed, plant out.
- Harvest when leaves have died back. Cook as for potatoes.

4.6 PRACTICAL TIPS FOR GROWING FRUIT VEGETABLES

VEGETABLES English *Spanish*	For salads (S) veget (V)	Grown from S* SD P	When - Autumn Winter Spring Summer A/W/Sp/S	Sow/plant in rows (R) blocks (B)
STEEM FRUITS				
Aubergines *Berenjenas*	V	S* P	LW/ESp Sp	- R
Pepper (sweet) *Pimientos (dulces)*	S/V	S* P	LW/ESp Sp	- R
Peppers - Padron *Pimientos de Padrón*	V	S* P*	ESp LSp	- R
Peppers - Hot *Pimientos guindillas*	V	S* P	LW/ESp Sp	- R
Peppers - chilli *Pimientos de cayenne*	V	S* P	LW/ESp Sp	- R
Pepper ornamental *Capsicum annum*	S	P*	ESp	- R
Tomatoes *Tomates*	SV	S* P	W/ESp Sp/S	- R
CURCUBITAS				
Courgettes *Calabacines*	V	S* P	LW/ESp Sp/ES	See below
Cucumbers *Pepinos*	S	S* P	LW/ESp Sp	R
Melon/cucumber *Melón/Pepino*	S	S* SD P	LW/ESp Sp Sp	R

Typical harvest times Autumn Winter Spring Summer A/W/Sp/S	Soil needs (1-8) & C	Extra feed needs N P K C M	Moisture needs High (H) Medium (M) Low (L)	Common pests and diseases (See Section 4.25) and other problems
S/A	1	P/M	H	Colorado beetle, wireworms. Fungal diseases
S/A	2	P	M	As above but not affected by Colorado beetle
S/A	2	P	M	As above
S/A/W	2	P	M	As above
S/A/W	2	P	M	As above
S/A	2	P	M	As above
Sp/S/A	1	P/M	M	As above. Bottom end rot. Tomatoes splitting when ripening due to irregular watering
LSp/S	4	N/P	H	Mildew and other fungal diseases. Spider mite
S	1/4/6	P	M	As above
S	2/6	P	M	As above

VEGETABLES **English** *Spanish*	**For salads (S) veget (V)**	**Grown from S* SD P**	**When - Autumn Winter Spring Summer A/W/Sp/S**	**Sow/plant in rows (R) blocks (B)**
CURCUBITAS				
Melons *Melones*	S/A	S* SD P	LW/ESp Sp Sp	 R
Water melons *Sandías*	S/V	S* SD P	LW/ESp Sp Sp	R
Pumpkins *Calabazas*	V	S* SD P	LW/ESp Sp Sp	 R
Squash *Calabazas*	S/V	S* SD P	LW/ESp Sp Sp	R
Gourds *Calabazas ornamentales*	Ornamental	S* SD	 Sp	 R
Butternut squash *Violines*	S/V	S* SD P	LW/ESp Sp Sp	 R
PULSES				
BEANS/JUDIAS				
Broad beans *Habas*	V	SD	A/EW	R/B
Butterbeans *Garrofón*	V	SD	L/Sp	R
French beans - Climbing *Judias enrame*	S/V	SD	Sp	R

Typical harvest times Autumn Winter Spring Summer A/W/Sp/S	Soil needs (1-8) & C	Extra feed needs N P K C M	Moisture needs High (H) Medium (M) Low (L)	Common pests and diseases (See Section 4.25) and other problems
S	4	P	L	As above
S/A	4	P	M	As above
S/A	4	P	M	As above
A/W	4	P	M	As above
S/A/W	4	P	M	As above
S/A	4	P	M	As above
Sp	5	-	L	Blackfly and blackspot
S/A	3	P	M	Blackfly, whitefly, red spider mite, bean weevils and fungal diseases
S	5	P	M	As above

VEGETABLES **English** *Spanish*	**For salads (S) veget (V)**	**Grown from S* SD P**	**When - Autumn Winter Spring Summer A/W/Sp/S**	**Sow/plant in rows (R) blocks (B)**
PULSES				
French beans - Dwarf *Judías bajo*	S/V	SD	Sp	R
Haricot/Lima beans *Judías tiernas/Alubias*	V	SD	Sp	R
Runner Beans *Peronas*	S/V	SD	Sp	R
Soya beans *Soya*	V	SD	Sp	R
String beans - climbing *Habichuelas*	V	SD	Sp +LS	R
PEAS				
Chickpeas *Garbanzos*	V	SD	LSp	R
Peas *Guisantes*	S/V	SD	LA	R
Petit-pois	S/V	SD	LA	R
Mangetout/Sugar snap *Cometodo/Tirabeques*	S/V	SD	LA	R
OTHERS				
Sweetcorn *Maíz dulce*	S/V	SD	Sp	R

Notes:
Esp = early spring.
LSp = late spring.
S = Seeds sown in containers - * plantlets planted out later.
SD = Seeds sown directly in ground.

Typical harvest times Autumn Winter Spring Summer A/W/Sp/S	**Soil needs (1-8) & C**	**Extra feed needs N P K C M**	**Moisture needs High (H) Medium (M) Low (L)**	**Common pests and diseases (See Section 4.25) and other problems**
S	5	P	M	As above
S	5	P	M	As above
S	3	P	M	As above
S/A	5	P	M	As above
S/A	3	P	M	As above
S/A	2	-	M	-
Sp	5	-	M	Pea weevil. Mildew
Sp	5	-	M	As above
Sp	5	-	M	As above
S/A	2	-	M	Aphids

P = Plantlets planted directly into the ground. *Can also be grown in pots.
N = high in nitrogen feed.
K = high in phosphorus/phosphate feed.
P = high in potassium/potash feed.
C = high in calcium (lime) feed.
M = mulch with comfrey leaves.

Soil needs

1. Soil enriched with plenty of manure/compost. Will tolerate partially decomposed/ fresh manure.
2. As above but all must be fully decomposed.
3. Trenches dug and filled with well-rotted manure/compost and capped with soil a month before sowing.
4. Large holes dug and filled with well-rotted/manure/compost during the previous winter.
5. Grows best in soil well enriched for preceding crops with no extra compost/manure added. Detest fresh compost.
6. Wood ash added to the soil before planting.
7. Grows best in soil enriched in nitrogen by previous pea and bean crops.
8. As soil 2 with added grit or coarse sand.

If you have not enriched your soil as in Section 4.3, you will need to resort to feeding all fruit plants with a granular or liquid general fertiliser high in potassium/potash weekly from the day you plant to the day you harvest vegetables that will need more than others are tomatoes, peppers, aubergines, cucumbers, courgettes, pumpkins and climbing beans. In all cases we recommend you use an ecological/organic food rather than manufactured chemicals.

OTHER TIPS

GENERAL

Fruit vegetables are the greatest sun-lovers of all the vegetables, so position them where they will have the maximum number of hours' sunshine throughout the day.

STEM FRUITS

When the first flowers start to form, reduce watering to avoid flower drop and increase the amount as soon as the fruits start to form to avoid stunted fruits.

Aubergines

- Varieties: dark red, purple to white, striped, round, elongated and oval.
- Harvest when fruits are a good size.
- Have a long harvesting period.

Sweet peppers

- Varieties: light greens which ripen to yellow/orange, others to red. Elongated (Italiano) and oval (Tres

Cantos) with mild sweet flavours are amongst the most popular.

• Harvest – either pick them the size you like them when they are still green or leave them to fully ripen. Gluts can be preserved by bottling (see Section 4.17).

Padrón peppers

• Harvest while small to fry in oil and garlic for a tasty tapa. Beware, the odd one can be 'very' hot. Especially those picked in the autumn.

Hot pepper *(guindilla)*

• Varieties: red and yellow.

• Reds dry to use in cooking. Yellows use in salads (with care!) and to conserve for winter.

Chilli peppers

• Varieties: numerous. Some hot and some lethal! Many colours and shapes.

• Harvest in late summer or early autumn when fully ripe. Hang them up in a cool, dry, shady terrace to dry. Use them as needed. Will keep for several years.

Ornamental peppers

• Produce small fruits of different colours, red, orange and yellow. Fairly hot.

Tomatoes

• Varieties: several hundred available in the seed catalogues. All shapes and sizes, from tiny cherry to Italian plum and enormous Spanish beefsteak. Colours vary from dark red to yellow. There are also trailing varieties that you can grow in your window box.

• Planting out: if they have become very leggy, plant the root deep with part of the stem laid horizontally across the base of the planting hole. Earth well up around the stem

to make the plant stable. To give them an extra boost of nitrogen and help them build up resistance to fungal diseases, place a few nettle leaves in the base of the planting hole.

- Harvest when they are fully ripe to use in salads, soups etc. If you have a glut, dry them in a dehydrator or bottle them in *a baño María* (bain-marie). The Spanish *"colgar"* variety is grown specifically for hanging and storing throughout the winter months. Pick the fruit just before they are fully ripe and hang up in a dry, covered, airy place. To retain storing properties, do not over water or over-feed with nitrogen.

CUCURBITAS

(name for the gourd family including courgettes, pumpkins, melons etc.)

To avoid fungal diseases, plant on low ridges and always water from below, never wetting the leaves, and keep them regularly lightly dusted with sulphur. To protect large-forming fruits from rotting or being eaten by slugs, place an appropriately sized, flat piece of wood underneath them before they get too big.

Courgettes

- Varieties: dark green, pale green to cream, long and round, mini and enormous.
- Harvest: pick while small for salads and to steam lightly unless you like big stuffed marrows. The more you pick them small the better the crop. If you have a glut, make chutney or purée to freeze as a base for soups. Some of the larger ones will store for a couple of months in a cool cellar.

Cucumber

- Varieties: we normally grow two types: the long English-style cucumber and the shorter, squat ridge cucumber which is like a large gherkin. Both supported on a frame.
- Gherkins can also be grown for using fresh or pickling.
- It's worth lightening the compost/manure mix by putting a little straw in their planting holes.

Melon-cucumber

- Variety: Alficoz. Tastes like its name and looks more like a cucumber. The plant is like a melon plant and the fruits grow either straight or curved.
- Harvest before the fruits get too large and bitter.

Melons

- Varieties typically grown include:
- Amarillo Oro and similar, soft yellow-skinned, oval, average taste, non-storing.
- Cantaloupe, average size, yellow and orange flesh, perfumed and sweet, non-storing, e.g. Sweetheart.
- Ogen, small to medium round, green to yellow, very sweet and tasty, non-storing, e.g. Blenheim orange.
- Hard-skinned ovals, very tasty and juicy, store well, e.g. Pinonet, *Piel de Sapo*.
- If you buy a really tasty melon in the supermarket, keep the seeds to plant. They need less water than pumpkins and squash. If there is no rain, water moderately every two weeks while the plant is growing. The less watering the sweeter and better keeping the fruit. In some areas where they have very deep, light, fertile soil such as in areas of La Mancha, they are grown dry, by flooding the land when planting and then with no further irrigation. Every two weeks they lift up the foliage and work the ground shallowly around the plants, being careful not to damage the fragile roots which grow very near to the surface.
- Harvesting. It is always hard to know when they are fully ripe. In the shops you see people comparing the weight of the larger hard-skinned varieties, picking up this one and that one and choosing the heaviest one of its size. If the top end feels soft under hard pressure, it is a good indication that it is ripe. Once harvested, seeds can be kept but hybrids are unlikely to reproduce faithfully.

Water melons

- Varieties: small round Sugar Baby to enormous motley green giants. Tasty dark red to white flesh.
- Harvest when the stem connection to the fruit starts to die back.
- Enjoy them as a cooling snack during the heat of the summer or, if you have a juicer, make a refreshing drink. Will store for a couple of months in a cool cellar.

Pumpkins, squash, butternut squash and gourds

- When planting out, allow one to two metres between plants — unless you are going for a record giant pumpkin when you will need five metres or more. To stimulate side branches, pinch out the end shoots when the plants are 50cm long.
- If you want a prize-winning giant pumpkin, when a few fruit have formed choose the one you want to continue growing and remove the remainder.
- Harvest when the stem connection to the fruit withers. Healthy undamaged fruits will store for up to 10 months in a cool dry cellar. All make interesting ornaments for the garden and terrace.

Pumpkins

- If you want to have fun and have the space, try and grow a record-sized "Atlantic Giant" — the largest have grown to 500 kilos in the USA. All you need is sun all day long, sheltered position, deep, manured planting holes and frequent supplementary feeds, water and plenty of space. Keep seeds from your harvest for next season. Our best effort so far is 60 kilos.
- Uses: to make soups, pies, bread or they can just be baked in the oven. Or just use them as ornaments around the garden. They will keep for several months.

Squash

- Varieties: many different shapes and sizes with skins from green to dark orange, mottled and smooth. The flesh inside varies from pale yellow to dark orange. The latter having the highest carotene content. Turk's Turban grows like its name and is multicoloured. The cabello de angel has a spaghetti-like centre which is cooked and used in preparing desserts, pastries and jams.
- Uses – as for pumpkins but they are generally sweeter. Store well in a cool dark cellar for up to a year. Turk's Turban has a milder flavour than some other varieties but is grown more for its very unusual decorative colours and shape.

Butternut squash

- Varieties – few.
- Uses – as for squash. Is a good substitute for carrot in carrot and apple juice as it is also very high in carotene. Peel it finely so as not to lose too much of the goodness.

Gourds

- Varieties – Many different shapes, sizes and colours.
- Not edible, grown for decoration of vegetable plot and terraces.
- Can be sun-dried and varnished.

PULSES

When the flowers start to form, reduce watering to avoid flower drop and, to avoid stunted fruits, increase the amount as soon as the fruits start to form.

BEANS

Hundreds of varieties exist, from dwarf to climbing, green , motley red to black, thin, long and narrow, rounded, straight, curved to wide and flat, stringless. The main types grown and uses are as follows:

Runner/climbing beans *(judías trepadoras or peronas)*

- Tall-growing beans like northern European runner beans in shape, but thinner, smoother and stringless. Varieties with pure green pods and green pods mottled with red splashes are grown. Both are sown in spring.
- Uses: for eating they are chopped into 5cm lengths and steamed as a vegetable, included in *cocidos* (meat stews) and *hervidos* (boiled vegetable starter), and one of the three bean ingredients of a genuine paella. Freeze well.
- Haricot/lima beans (judías tiernas, alubias)
- Red and white varieties. Both dwarf and tall varieties are sown in the spring.
- Uses: steamed and eaten very young or dried for winter use and used in a wide variety of regional dishes. For drying, leave in the pod on the plant and then dry further in a covered area.

Dwarf and climbing French beans *(judías enrama, frijoles, judías bajas, enanas)*

- Sown in the spring.
- Uses: eaten fresh in salads or steamed as a regular vegetable. Some dwarf grow purple but turn green on cooking. Freeze well.

Long string beans *(judías verdes, habichuelas)*

- Sown in late spring and sometimes mid-summer to give a later crop.
- Harvest when young. Use in soups, stews and *arroz al horno* (oven-cooked rice dish) and steam as a vegetable. If you have a glut, conserve in *a baño maría* (bain-marie). Those that are suitable for drying harvest in early autumn. Allow pods to dry out completely then pod beans and store in airtight containers. To kill off any weevils freeze dried beans for a couple of days before you store them.

Butter beans *(judías garrofón)*

- Sown in late spring.
- Pinch out tips of flower heads as they form to encourage larger beans.
- Grow on a tunnel support (see Section 5.1), so that the forming beans can hang down in the shade and for easier access when pinching out.
- Harvest young when the beans have just formed in the pod and use raw in salads or when bigger cooked fresh in Valencian paellas, *arroz al horno* and stews and dried for later use. The pods can be left on the plants until the autumn and the beans can then be dried and stored over winter as beans above.

Soya beans *(habas de soja)*

- Sown in spring.
- Uses: steamed as a vegetable, added to salads or dried for use as a sprouting bean or ground into soya flour used in soups and breads. Can also be left on plant and dried as beans above.

Broad beans *(habas)*

• Sown successionally in September, October and November.

• Harvest when young and eat raw as a tapa or in a salad, as they mature steam as a vegetable or fried with slivers of jamón serrano and garlic for a tasty tapa. The whole pod can be used when small and tender. Can also be dried and stored over winter.

Peas

• Varieties: many to choose from. Some low growing that don't need staking and others that can grow as tall as climbing beans. From tiny sweet petit pois to larger, tasty heavy croppers such as Rondo. On the packets look for *"mata baja"* (low-growing) and *"enrame mata alta"* (tall and needs staking).

• Sow in early winter so that they are finished cropping before the weather heats up, to avoid mildew.

• Harvest when young. Use raw in salads, cook by steaming and freeze if you have a glut.

Mangetout, sugar snap eat-all peas

• Will need staking as they grow tall.

• Harvest when really young before pods start to get stringy and the peas start to form in the pod. Steam the pods lightly. They do not freeze well.

• When sugar snap peas get too large to eat as mangetout, leave on the plant until the peas are fully formed and harvest as normal peas.

OTHER

Sweetcorn

• Varieties: for a really sweet cob buy those in packets marked *"maíz dulce"*. There are multicoloured varieties but they don't eat well. There are others in UK mail order catalogues. You can also buy loose from animal feed shops but it has little taste and is used essentially for feeding animals. We plant it around the plot to attract unwanted insects away from other plants.

Never plant different varieties near each other.

• Grows well inter-planted with climbing beans. They provide nitrogen and the corn the necessary support.

• Harvest in late summer and autumn when the cobs' outside leaves have dried off. Cook by steaming or boiling until tender and drizzle with olive oil.

4.7 PRACTICAL TIPS FOR GROWING LEAF CROPS INCLUDING HERBS

VEGETABLES **English** *Spanish*	**For salads (S) veget (V) Flavour (F)**	**Grown from Seeds S* SD** P C/R**	**When - Autumn Winter Spring Summer A/W/Sp/S**	**Sow/plant in rows (R) blocks (B)**
BRASSICAS				
Brussel sprouts *Coles de Bruselas*	SV	S*/SD** P	ES LS	R/B
Cabbages *Coles*	S/V	S*/SD** P	LS A	R/B
Red cabages *Coles lombardas*	S/V	S*/SD** P	LS A	R/B
Cauliflowers *Coliflores*	S/V	S*/SD** P	LS A	R/B
Channel Islands walking stick kale	V and for walking sticks	S*SD** P	LS A	R/B
Kale - curly *Berza rizada*	V	SD* P	LS A	R/B
Kohlrabi *Colinabos*	S/V	SD**	LSp/LS/ A	R/B
LEAFY AND ORIENTAL SALADS				
Cut and come again salad leaves	S	S*/SD** P	LS/A/LW A/EW/Sp	R/B
Chicory *Escarola*	S	S*/SD** P	LS/A/LW/ A/AE/Sp	R/B
Land cress *Berro de la tierra*	S	S*/SD** P	LS/A/LW A/EW/Esp	R/B

Typical harvest times Autumn Winter Spring Summer A/W/Sp. S	Soil needs (1-8) & C	Extra feed needs N P K C M	Moisture needs High (H) Medium (M) Low (L)	Common pests and diseases (See Section 5.7) and other problems
W/Sp	5/7	-	M	Aphids, caterpillars, club root, wireworm
LW/ESp	2/7	-	M	As above
LW/ESp	2/7	-	M	As above
LW/ESp	2/7	-	M	As above
LW/ESp	2/7	N	M	As above
LW/ESp	2/7	-	M	As above
A/W/Sp	2/7	-	M	-
A/W/Sp/ES	5	-	M	Slugs and snails
A/W/Sp/ES	2/7	-	H	As above
A/W/Sp/ES	5	-	M	As above

VEGETABLES **English** *Spanish*	**For salads (S) veget (V) Flavour (F)**	**Grown from Seeds S* SD** P C/R**	**When - Autumn Winter Spring Summer A/W/Sp/S**	**Sow/plant in rows (R) blocks (B)**
LEAFY AND ORIENTAL SALADS				
Lettuces *Lechugas*	S/V	S*/SD** P	LS/A/LW A/EW/ESp	R/B
Mustard greens - Red giant	S/V	S*/SD**P	LS/A/LW A/EW/ESp	R/B
Pak choi	S/V	S*/SD**P	LS/A/LW A/EW/ESp	R/B
Rocket *Oruga*	S/V	SD	LS/A/LW/ Sp	R/B
OTHERS				
Asparagus *Espárrago*	S/V	SD** P	LS/LW/ESp A/Sp	R
Cardoon *Cardo*	V	P	LS/LW	R
Fennel *Hinojo*	S/V	SD** P	LS/LW A/ESp	R/B
Leeks *Puerros*	S/V	S*/SD** P	LS/LW/Sp A/LW/Sp/LS	R/B
Spinach *Espinaca*	S/V	S*/SD** P	LS/LW A/EW/ESp	R/B
Swiss chard *Acelgas*	V	S*/SD** P	LS A/EW	R/B
Okra *Kimbombo*	V	S*/SD** P	ESp LSp	R
HERBS				
Anise *Anís*	F	S*/SD** P	Sp SpS	R/B

Typical harvest times Autumn Winter Spring Summer A/W/Sp. S	Soil needs (1-8) & C	Extra feed needs N P K C M	Moisture needs High (H) Medium (M) Low (L)	Common pests and diseases (See Section 5.7) and other problems
A/W/Sp/ES	5	N	M	As above
A/W/Sp/ES	5	N	M	As above
A/W/Sp/ES		N	M	As above
A/W/Sp/ES	5	N	M	As above
LW/Sp	1	-	M	Asparagus beetle. Rust
A/Sp	2	-	H	Slugs and snails
All year	2	-	M	-
All year	2	N/K	L	Rust
A/W/Sp/ES	5	N/K as a foliar feed	L	Blackfly and snails
W/SP	2/7	N/K	M	Blackfly
S	2	-	M	-
S/A	2	-	M	-

VEGETABLES English *Spanish*	For salads (S) veget (V) Flavour (F)	Grown from Seeds S* SD** P C/R	When - Autumn Winter Spring Summer A/W/Sp/S	Sow/plant in rows (R) blocks (B)
HERBS				
Basil *Albahaca*	S/F	S*/SD** P*	Sp Sp	R/B
Borage *Borraja*	V	SD** P	L/W/ESp A/Sp	R/B
Chamomile Matricaria *Manzanilla*		S*SD* P*	LS/Esp A/Sp	R/B
Comfrey *Consuelda*	Fertiliser	R	W/ESp	R/B
Coriander *Cilandro*	F	S*SD P*	Sp Sp	R/B
Cumin *Comino*	F	S*/SD** P*	Sp Sp	R/B
Dandelion *Diente de león*	S/V	SD	LS/A/Sp	R/B
Dill *Eneldo*	F	S*/SD P*	Sp Sp	R/B
Marjoram *Orégano*	S/F	S*/SD** P*	ESp Sp	R/B
Parsley *Perejil*	S/V	S*/SD** P*	LS/LW	R/B
Peppermint *Piperita*	S/F	S*/SD P/R*	Esp Sp	R/B
Purslane *Verdelaga*	S	SD	LS/LW	R/B
Rosemary *Romero*	F	P* C	All year	R/B

Typical harvest times Autumn Winter Spring Summer A/W/Sp. S	Soil needs (1-8) & C	Extra feed needs N P K C M	Moisture needs High (H) Medium (M) Low (L)	Common pests and diseases (See Section 5.7) and other problems
Sp/S/A	2	-	H	Slugs and snails
A/Sp	2	-	L	-
Sp/S	2	-	M	-
LSp/S/A EW	1	N/K	H	-
Sp/S/leaf A seeds	2	-	M	-
S/A seeds	2	-	M	-
A/EW/Sp	5	-	M	-
Sp/S/leaf A seeds	2	-	M	-
All year	8	-	L	-
All year	2	-	H	-
S/AEW/Sp	2	-	M	Grown in container buried in the ground to stop roots being evasive
A/Sp/S	5	-	M	-
All year	8	-	L	-

VEGETABLES **English** *Spanish*	**For salads (S) veget (V) Flavour (F)**	**Grown from Seeds S* SD** P C/R**	**When - Autumn Winter Spring Summer A/W/Sp/S**	**Sow/plant in rows (R) blocks (B)**
HERBS				
Rue *Ruda*	I	P*	A/Sp	R/B
Sage *Salvia*	F	P/C/R	A/Sp	R/B
Sorrel *Acedera*	S/V	SD**	LS/LW	R/B
Tarragon *Estragón*	S/F	S*SD** P* C	LS/ESp A/Sp	R/B
GREEN MANURES				
Phacellia *Facelia*	-	S/Direct	LS	B
Alfalfa *Alfalfa*	-	S/Direct	LS	B

Notes:
ESp = Early spring etc.
LSp = Late spring etc.
S = Seeds sown in containers, *plantlets planted out later.
SD = Seeds sown directly in ground.
*Need thinning out. **Thinnings can be transplanted.
P = Plantlets planted directly in ground.
*Can be grown in pots.
C = Grown by taking cuttings
R = Multiplied by root division.
*Can be grown in pots.
N = High in nitrogen feed.
P = High in phosphorus/phosphate feed.
K = High in potassium/potash feed.
C = C high in calcium feed (lime).
M = Mulch with comfrey leaves.

Typical harvest times Autumn Winter Spring Summer A/W/Sp. S	Soil needs (1-8) & C	Extra feed needs N P K C M	Moisture needs High (H) Medium (M) Low (L)	Common pests and diseases (See Section 5.7 and other problems)
All year	8	-	L	-
All year	8	-	L	Mealy bug
All year round	5	-	M	Slugs and snails
A/Sp/S	2	-	M	Slugs and snails
LW/ESp	-	-	M	-
LW/ESp	-	-	M	-

Soil needs:

1. Soil enriched with plenty of manure/compost. Will tolerate partially decomposed/fresh manure.
2. As above, but all must be fully decomposed.
3. Trenches dug and filled with well-rotted manure/compost and capped with soil a month before sowing.
4. Large holes dug and filled with well-rotted/manure/compost during the previous winter.
5. Grows best in soil well-enriched for preceding crops with no extra compost/manure added. Detests fresh compost.
6. Wood ash added to the soil before planting.
7. Grows best in soil enriched in nitrogen by previous pea and bean crops.
8. As soil 2 with added grit or coarse sand.

If you have not enriched your soil as in Section 4 .3, you will need to resort to feeding all leaf vegetables with a granular or liquid general fertiliser high in nitrogen weekly from the day you plant to the day you harvest. In all cases we recommend you use a natural ecological/organic feed rather than manufactured chemicals.

OTHER TIPS

A. BRASSICAS

Brussels sprouts

• To produce compact sprouts, firm in well around plantlets when planting. For a continuous crop, pick regularly and remove lower leaves.

Cabbages

• We normally grow only one crop to harvest in late winter/early spring mainly because we don't have to water so much. Cabbages withstand cold temperatures and are out of the ground before it gets too hot and they go to seed. But, depending on your microclimate, you can sow seeds in trays in the greenhouse in late winter, transplant in early spring for harvesting in early summer or sow seeds directly in seedbed in spring, transplant late summer and harvest early winter. If growing from seed, look for varieties suitable for the various seasons, otherwise the plantlets for sale in your area would be the most suitable.

• Keep soil around stems earthed up to help support the plant when it gets top-heavy.

• Hoe and mulch between rows with well-rotted compost.

• Cabbages can withstand fairly dry conditions but obviously do better when regularly watered.

Cauliflowers

• We grow cauliflowers according to the lunar calendar (see section 4.15) in the leaf phase as if they are grown as a flower vegetable they don't form good tight heads and go to seed much faster.
• When transplanting, plant up to the base of the first leaves, being careful not to get any soil into the centre of the plants.
• In hot weather, when heads are forming, fold over outer leaves to protect the heads from the sun.
• If you have a glut, you can store by lifting with roots, removing soil and hanging with heads downwards in a cool cellar. Spray with water regularly to keep fresh.
• As they cannot tolerate dry conditions, keep soil around plants well-worked and never let it become hard-packed.
• For an earlier crop sow seed direct into seed bed in late spring, transplanting in late summer to harvest in late autumn.

Channel Islands walking stick kale

• Grown for fun. Leaves are okay if eaten young. Dried tall stems last for years as walking sticks or in our case keeping the gate open.

Curly kale

• Again we prefer to grow it for harvesting in late winter and early spring. But it is a very useful winter crop if you live in colder climes. Therefore, sow in seed beds in mid-summer and transplant in early autumn to harvest during the winter months.

Kohlrabi

• Sow direct into ground and thin out if necessary. They don't transplant well.
• So that you don't have a glut, sow seeds every couple of weeks.

B. LEAFY AND ORIENTAL SALADS

a. Cut-and-come-again. Many varieties, such as lamb's lettuce, spicy oriental salad leaves, mustard green giant and saladini. You will find others in UK seed catalogues. These are good crops for window boxes and containers as they take up little room, grow and can be harvested over a long period.

b. Lettuces. Winter/early spring varieties: trocadero with compact, strong pale green leaves; *maravilla de cuatro estaciones* with dark-green reddish leaves; Roman type, upright with soft, wrinkled leaves and a compact heart, does not need tying up. There are also several varieties of green or red oak leaf lettuces which taste good and look very decorative on a salad plate.

Summer varieties: batavia *(maravilla de verano)* has a tight compact cabbage-like head, good resistance to heat but benefits from shading during very hot weather; Iceberg, crinkly leaves and good tight head. Both varieties can also be grown in the winter.
• To avoid fungal problems when transplanting, don't plant any deeper than they were in seed beds.
• Although a feed of liquid manure and nettle is beneficial, don't overdo it as your plants will grow too fast.
• As they need plenty of water, mulch and hoe between rows to retain moisture.

- Pick cut-and-come-again salads and other greens such as rocket regularly to stop them going to seed and to encourage young tasty shoots.

C. OTHERS

Asparagus

- Easy to grow from seed but you will have to wait three to four years to pick your first harvest. Alternatively, you can buy plantlets to plant in the autumn or spring to harvest in two years. Don't be tempted to cut any spears that appear in the first year. The plant needs to build up a stronger root system before you start harvesting in earnest. Even then leave several spears on each plant to grow to maturity.
- Fern-like foliage will form. In the autumn when it dies back cut the stems down to the ground level so the sap goes back down into the roots, strengthening the plant.
- Over winter, while dormant, cover the raised beds with a good layer of rotted compost and seaweed. There is no need to wash off the salt as asparagus loves salt. Perhaps that is why they grow so well near the sea. In fact, feeding them with 50g of sea salt per square metre at the end of April is beneficial. Do it on a rainy day or water in well.

Cardoon

- A very popular perennial vegetable eaten by the Spaniards. Same family as the artichoke but grown for its stems and decorative flowers.
- To harvest, pick off outside leaves as you need them. Shave off the outer green leaf. Boil in water, changing it twice to remove some of the bitterness and cook until soft. Strain and marinate with olive oil and crushed garlic. Serve as a *tapa* or add to your salad. The Spanish use it mostly in vegetable and meat casseroles.

Fennel

- Fennel is easy to grow and requires little attention apart from regular watering, hoeing and mulching around plants.
- Seedlings can be transplanted bare rooted.
- Pick the bulbs young to eat raw in salads or leave to grow larger to steam as a vegetable. By cutting them off at the base they will continuously re-sprout for many months.
- If they go to seed in the height of the summer, use the seed heads to attract insects off other plants.
- In late summer harvest the dried seeds to use in cooking or as a refreshing infusion.
- Cut the whole plant down to the base after it has seeded and if it gets caught by heavy frost. It will soon start to sprout again.
- Each year sow a few new plants as they need replacing after about three years.

Leeks

- Keep soil around plants hoed and mulched.
- You cut off the top third of green leaf when planting out but you can do the same when they are growing strongly to encourage more growth into the lower stems.
- If you have initially planted them into deep holes with tops just showing, you should not need to blanch them further by earthing up around the stems.
- Use thinnings to eat raw in salads.

Spinach

- Although it does not need a lot of water still likes to be kept evenly moist.
- Would benefit from some shading in the summer. This is why we prefer to grow it in the cooler winter months.
- To harvest, either dig up the whole plant or pick off outside leaves to prolong harvest.

Swiss chard

- As above, but harvest by pulling off outside stems as you need them. Leaves and stems can be cooked separately.

Okra

- Harvest when young. Gets tough quickly.

C. HERBS

Grow them on the vegetable plot for these reasons:

a. As companion plants attracting beneficial insects — allow them to flower as long as possible.

b. As additional main ingredients in salads — cut as required.

c. In small amounts for flavouring — cut as required.

d. Anise, chamomile, dandelion, peppermint, sage, rosemary and rue make useful infusions.

D. GREEN MANURES

Cut and work into ground by digging in or rotavating.

4.8 PRACTICAL TIPS FOR GROWING FLOWER VEGETABLES AND USEFUL COMPANION PLANTS

VEGETABLES **English** *Spanish*	**For salads (S) veget (V)**	**Grown from Seeds S* SD** P C**	**When - Autumn Winter Spring Summer A/W/Sp/S**	**Sow/plant in rows (R) blocks (B)**
FLOWER VEGETABLES				
Artichokes-globe *Alcachofas*	SV	SD** P C	LS/LW LW/ESp LS/LW	R/B
Brocolli-sprouting *Brecol*	S/V	S*/SD** P	LS A	R/B
Calabrese *Calabrese*	S/V	S*/SD** P	LS A	R/B
Capers *Alcaparra*	S	S	Sp/S	R/B
Romanesco *Romanesque*	S/V	S*SD** P	LS A	R/B
Sunflower *Girasol*	S	S*/SD*	LS	R
COMPANION PLANTS				
Chrysanthemum *Crisantemo*	-	S* P C	LW/ESp Sp LW/ESp	R/B
Marigolds *Calendula*	-	SD**	LS/LW ESp	R/B
Nasturtium *Capuchina*	S	SD**	LW/ESp	R/B

Typical harvest times Autumn Winter Spring Summer A/W/Sp. S	Soil needs (1-8) & C	Extra feed needs N P K C M	Moisture needs High (H) Medium (M) Low (L)	Common pests and diseases (See Section 5.7) and other problems
Sp/ES	1	K	H	Blackfly, slugs and snails
W/ESp	2	K	M	Whitefly
W/ESp	2	K	M	As above
Sp/S	8	-	L	-
LW/ESp	2	K	M	As above
S/A	2	-	M	-
A/W	2	K	M	Aphids
Sp/ES/A/W	2	K	M	Blackfly (CP)
Sp/A	2	K	H	Slugs and snails Blackfly (CP)

VEGETABLES **English** *Spanish*	**For salads (S) veget (V)**	**Grown from Seeds S* SD** P* C***	**When - Autumn Winter Spring Summer A/W/Sp/S**	**Sow/plant in rows (R) blocks (B)**
COMPANION PLANTS				
Rosemary *Romero*	S	P/C	All year	R/B
Borage *Borraje*	S/V	SD**	LW/ESp	R/B
Sage *Salvia*	S	P/C	A/Sp	R/B
Sweet peas *Guisante de olor*	-	SD	EW	R
Roses *Rosales*	-	P/C	A/W/Sp	R

Notes:
A. ESp = early spring etc.
LSp = late spring etc.
S = Seeds sown in containers. *Plantlets planted out later.
SD = Seeds sown directly in ground. *Need thinning out.
**Thinnings can be ransplanted.
P = Plantlets planted directly in ground.
C = Grown by taking cuttings or offshoots and planting directly in ground.
N = high in nitrogen feed.
P = high in phosphorus/phosphate feed.
K = high in potassium/potash feed.
C = high in calcium feed (lime).
M = mulch with comfrey leaves.

Soil needs:
1. Soil enriched with plenty of manure/compost. Will tolerate partially decomposed/fresh manure.
2. As above but all must be fully decomposed.
3. Trenches dug and filled with well-rotted manure/compost and capped with soil a month before sowing.

Typical harvest times Autumn Winter Spring Summer A/W/Sp. S	Soil needs (1-8) & C	Extra feed needs N P K C M	Moisture needs High (H) Medium (M) Low (L)	Common pests and diseases (See Section 4.25) and other problems
All year	8	-	L	-
A/Sp/S	2	-	L	-
All year	8	-	L	-
Sp/ES	2	K	M	-
Sp/S/A/EW	1+6	K/C Seaweed	H	Black spot, rust, mildew, aphids

4. Large holes dug and filled with well-rotted/manure/compost during the previous winter.
5. Grows best in soil well enriched for preceding crops with no extra compost/manure added. Detests fresh compost.
6. Wood ash added to the soil before planting.
7. Grows best in soil enriched in nitrogen by previous pea and bean crops.
8. As soil 2 with added grit or coarse sand.

If you have not enriched your soil as in Section 4.3, you will need to resort to feeding all flower vegetables with a granular or liquid general fertiliser high in potassium with some phosphorus and nitrogen weekly, from the day you plant to the day you harvest. Vegetables that will need more than others are broccoli, calabrese, romanesque, sweet peas and roses. In all cases we recommend you use a natural ecological/organic feed rather than manufactured chemicals.

FLOWER VEGETABLES

OTHER TIPS

Artichokes (globe)

- Varieties: few.

• Harvest while the hearts are well formed and firm. Once you have cut out the centre heart, smaller hearts will form on the lateral branches. Prepare by cutting off the tougher outside petals leaving the centre tender crown, or leave whole. Steam or boil until well cooked and serve as a tapa dressed in olive oil and crushed garlic.

Broccoli and calabrese

• Varieties: broccoli, green and purple sprouting varieties including a small wok brok variety; calabrese, many green sprouting varieties, similar to broccoli but more prolific. You will find many more in UK seed catalogues.

• Harvest. Cut out the top central flower first when it is well formed and before it starts going to seed. Then the plants will start to sprout from the side branches. Pick regularly to encourage new growth and stop them going to seed. Cook tender shoots steamed lightly and dressed with olive oil or best of all eat raw in salads or with a dip.

Capers

• Need heat. Grow best from Almería south. Prefer sandy/calcium high soils and like to get roots under/between rocks.

• The flower buds are picked for use in salads, fresh or pickled.

Romanesque

• Variety – few.

• Harvesting. The broccoli/cauliflower-type heads can grow large but it is best to harvest them before they get too big and start to go to seed. Some side shoots may continue to grow, but it crops more like a cauliflower than broccoli. Cook as for broccoli above.

Sunflowers

• Varieties – single and multi-flowered heads. Colours: reds, yellows, creams, from small to towering Russian giants.

• Harvest. Cut when all the petals have died off, the seeds have formed and before the birds eat them. Dry them in the sun and then remove seeds and store in an airtight container. Roast them in salt ready to eat as snacks, or if you have patience shell some and add to salads, or just feed the whole head to the chickens or hang up for wild birds. Keep some seeds to sow the following spring.

COMPANION PLANTS

Most of those listed in the table above can be grown from seed.

- Varieties: limited choice. For a wider choice, especially for chrysanthemums, sage and sweet peas, use a UK catalogue.

Garden centres now stock a good selection of sage.

Roses

- A good choice of local varieties, but for the more exotic we have ordered from UK growers. We have equal success with growing local varieties as with imported varieties.
- Grown to attract pollinators as well as for brightening up the vegetable plot and for cutting.
- To improve their scent, add dried blood to your feeds in the spring and put slices of onion and banana skins in the soil beside the plants monthly.
- Apart from cut flowers, why not make some rosewater. Pick three or four of your favourite red, scented blooms, take them apart, put in a saucepan with a litre of water, bring to boil and then simmer for 15 minutes. Filter and bottle when cool. Will keep in a cool place for a couple of weeks.
- A garlic planted alongside each helps protect against fungal problems. Indeed, you can grow your entire garlic crops among the roses.

4.9 DECIDING WHAT TO GROW YOURSELF

Part Three will have already helped you to decide on the style of your vegetable garden and the growing area of your chosen plot.

The tables in the preceding sections 4.5 to 4.8 have listed almost 90 types of vegetables that you could grow in Spain. Multiply that figure by the number of easily accessible varieties of each that could be grown and your choice runs into hundreds. Sources of seeds are discussed in Section 4.12.

Summer water restrictions will restrict or even prevent the growing of vegetables during the summer months as living in a frost belt or above the snow line can restrict winter cultivation and how early you can plant out in the spring. But for most gardeners the choice is yours. We suggest you make your choice along these lines:

1. Aim to grow a diversity of crops for interest and health benefits.
2. First decide on the vegetables that you most like and perhaps miss.
3. Include those vegetables that you have difficulty in purchasing as fresh as you like or are exorbitantly expensive when they are first available.
4. If space allows, include the whole spectrum of salad vegetables and herbs.
5. Provide for a range of staple seasonal vegetables so as to be able to ring the changes.
6. Recognise that, since some vegetables mature faster than others, some parts of your soil can be planted up numerous times a year.
7. If short of space, or you have cold springs or very hot late summers, or don't want the fuss of growing everything from seed, purchase plantlets as discussed in Sections 4.10 and 4.11.

4.10 BENEFITS OF STARTING WITH PLANTLETS

You have prepared your soil, decided what vegetables to grow and now is the time to decide whether to start by planting plantlets rather than by sowing seeds. Plantlets are young plants mature enough and hardened off enough to transplant from a nursery greenhouse or outdoor bed into a permanent container, raised bed or vegetable plot etc., to grow onto maturity. There are several benefits in doing this:

1. If you don't have experience of growing from seed in the Spanish climate, it makes sense to take advantage for little cost of others' experience of doing so over many years.

You may decide to grow some or all of your own later when you have more time and understand your Spanish soil and seasonal climates.

2. Plantlets can save you several months or indeed weeks of growing to plantlet size from seed. If you don't buy plantlets, you may miss a total growing season, autumn/winter or spring/summer because the temperatures are already unsuitable to start sowing seeds, i.e. too cold in early winter or too hot in early summer.

3. By growing vegetables from plantlets you raise the productivity of your plot because you only have to accommodate the plants for perhaps 60 to 80 per cent of their life cycle. If you replace harvested mature plants with new plantlets as soon as there are spaces, you grow up to 25 per cent more vegetables a year compared with sowing seeds directly into the ground.

4. Plantlets for many traditional proven varieties of vegetables can be purchased inexpensively at many garden centres, horticultural shops, local markets, agricultural cooperatives and the "greenhouse cities" of the major commercial plantlet growers who supply large-scale agriculturists. The latter normally sell retail as a side line.

5. You avoid the time, effort and sometimes the frustration of growing from seed — especially for varieties that are difficult to germinate reliably. You don't have the uncertainty of having to wait to see whether a packet of seeds is going to germinate successfully and grow into strong seedlings.

6. You can buy as many or as few plants as you want and won't need to worry about what to do with excess plantlets, which often occurs if you grow from seed.

7. It's possible to try out new varieties of vegetables by buying just two or three plantlets.

8. In some cases they will have been raised organically even if you have yet to change over totally to organic practices.

9. You can grow some early or out-of-season crops by planting plantlets under plastic cloches earlier than you could raise them from seed in the open ground.

10. Availability for sale of specific types of plantlets is a good indication that this is the season when Spaniards traditionally plant out that type of vegetable in a particular area.

11. You can grow your own plantlets from seed in a greenhouse in order to have plantlets to plant out when others are only just able to sow seed in the open ground.

12. In some cases, such as onions, leeks and lettuces, it is convenient to grow your own plantlets in a dedicated open-air bed where it is easier to control weeds and water appropriately than if you sowed more thinly in final situations on the main vegetable-growing areas.

13. You may have a failure with a sowing in a greenhouse, seed bed or main growing area. Plantlets are a quick way of solving such problems.

Other factors affecting the productivity of your vegetable growing will be discussed in later sections.

The two drawbacks of only buying plantlets is that it restricts the diversity of vegetable varieties that you will be able to grow and the seeds used by the supplier will rarely be organic. We therefore look at growing vegetables from seed in Sections 4.12 and 4.13.

Our growing strategy is a combination of buying plantlets, raising our own plantlets and of growing from seed sown directly into a final growing situation with no transplanting.

4.11 BUYING PLANTLETS

There are two main seasons for buying plantlets: late winter/early spring and in the autumn/early winter. At these times you will find plantlets available in garden centres, local markets, horticultural shops, agricultural cooperatives and major green house complexes that grow plantlets by the million for commercial vegetable growers in Spain as well as for export. If you're lucky you'll also find them at local smallholdings. Unfortunately, with the encroachment of new housing developments into rural land, many of these are disappearing.

With luck you will find a good range of seasonal plantlets of varieties. However, the choice will not be as diverse as the range of vegetables listed in sections 4.5 to 4.8, nor will the number of varieties of each type. There are a number of reasons for this.

a. Some types of vegetables do not transplant well.

b. Not all the vegetables popular in Northern Europe have been traditionally grown in Spain. Locals often ask us: "Whatever are you growing there?"

c. Spaniards are excellent at cooking a few vegetables in many tasty ways compared to the UK where it is more normal to cook a wider range of vegetables.

d. Spaniards have never had the tradition of breeding numerous varieties and even now many keep from year to year seeds of the 10 or so vegetable varieties that the family has grown for generations. Also the range of seeds available from Spanish seed merchants is smaller than in the UK. They have been rationalised in recent years to concentrate on the faster-selling lines grown by commercial growers. For instance, there are several hundred varieties/cultivars of tomatoes available to the amateur gardener in Spain from overseas mail order catalogues, but you will find few in Spanish seed displays and even fewer in the plantlets for sale.

e. Spaniards do not generally have access to mail order catalogues of the type issued by Thompson and Morgan or the Organic Gardening Catalogue in the UK. But you can obtain them to import seeds for your own sowings. A list of such suppliers is given in Section 4.12.

But don't despair. You will find sufficient varieties to make a good start and increasingly they are being grown according to ecological and organic principles. Although we grow many varieties of vegetables from seed, we still buy plantlets if we see something interesting or have not had time to raise all the seeds we intended while finishing off this book or to evaluate what is being offered for sale.

When you go to buy plantlets, you will find that they are sold: singly in individual pots; in modular trays of 100 or 200 plantlets for smaller plants or trays of 20 or 30 of larger plants that can be split; in small quantities removed from the modular trays and wrapped in newspaper; and dug up from nursery beds and sold singly or as with onions in bunches of 200 or 300 plantlets.

All methods are quite acceptable. But do ensure that you obtain plantlets that:

- have good root balls that have been kept damp and not allowed to dry out
- are compact and not unduly leggy
- show no signs of disease or pests
- have not been damaged
- are obviously not the end of the day's stock, other gardeners having already purchased the stronger plants
- have been hardened off. If not, ensure you harden them off, initially in a cold greenhouse or cold frame and then gradually putting them outside during the day and eventually also the nights as temperatures rise. If you have purchased plantlets a few weeks early for your situation, it is worth potting them up in plant pots for a few weeks to grow into stronger plants before planting them out. The issue is obviously more of a problem in the spring than in the autumn.

When your collection of plantlets is being assembled and packed, ensure that you label them well so that you don't muddle them when you come to plant them.

When you arrive home, wrap up each type/variety in dampened newspaper and label again. Then immediately place in a bucket or bowl with a little water at the bottom until you have time to plant out. But don't leave for too many days or roots and delicate leaves can start to rot.

Good plantlets will soon get going and before long the first harvest will be on the table at breakfast, lunch and dinner time. But, once you have become used to the Spanish climate, do have a go at growing your own plantlets from seed. As explained in the next section this is not difficult.

4.12 GROWING YOUR OWN PLANTLETS

Reasons for growing your own

As already discussed purchasing plantlets is a productive way of starting to grow vegetables on a mini, small or larger scale.

However there are five advantages of growing your own.

- You can grow a wider variety of types and cultivars of vegetables and herbs than normally available from commercial growers of plantlets.
- You can grow your plantlets earlier or later according to your particular microclimate.
- If you plan to use the lunar calendar, you can be sure that your seeds are sown on the most beneficial dates. See Section 4.15.
- If you plan to grow organically, you control what seeds, fertilisers, insecticides and fungicides are used in growing the plantlets.
- It is very satisfying to raise your own strong healthy plantlets and eventually harvest your own crops.

This section outlines where seeds can be obtained and how they can be sown and raised most effectively. The guidelines will help avoid beginners' mistakes.

Benefits of starting seeds in containers

In theory all seeds can be sown directly into raised beds or a vegetable plot. However, in practice this is sometimes difficult in Spain and also would not make the maximum use of your growing space. The reasons:

- In Spain there can be wide variations between night and day temperatures which can make it difficult to achieve consistent good germination and the continuous growth of seedlings.
- The heat of a propagator or greenhouse may be required to start those seeds needing a high and constant temperature to germinate.
- Hot and cold winds can soon dry out seedbeds.
- Torrential rain and hail can wash young seeds out of the ground.
- Even if not washed out young seedlings can become waterlogged.
- It is beneficial to achieve the earliest and longest growing period for many summer crops. It is therefore necessary to sow early tomatoes, peppers, aubergines, melons, squash etc. inside during the period December to March (depending on your location) when the weather in most areas can be too cold for germinating seeds. By growing inside optimum temperatures and soil moisture levels can be achieved.
- Strong plantlets can be planted out when the weather warms up in the spring.
- Similarly, to get winter crops such as brassicas, winter lettuces, spinach and onions off to a good start in the autumn it is best to sow their seeds in the shade during July and August as emergent seedlings in the open ground can be easily scorched. The plantlets can then be planted out from September to November when the weather has cooled down and with luck there have been autumn rains.
- Many of the annual herbs that we regard as vegetables are easier to raise first in pots or trays.
- Emerging seedlings can be attacked overnight by slugs and snails.
- In dry conditions ants can carry away seeds.
- Saves the problem of trying to weed between slow-growing varieties such as parsnips, carrots, onions and leeks.
- When planted out, they can be spaced productively with no gaps where seeds failed to germinate.
- Seedbeds will not be disturbed by cats, dogs or other predators. Mice have a habit of collecting peas for winter hibernation and likewise foraging pigeons love a feast.
- If your vegetable plot is away from the house, you can't keep a close watch on your seedbeds.
- In very wet or cold conditions you won't be able to prepare the soil or sow seeds so the best lunar calendar sowing dates will be missed unless you sow in containers.

SUCCESS FACTORS FOR GROWING YOUR OWN PLANTLETS

a. Seed selection and purchasing

Buy from suppliers that have a regular turnover of seeds to ensure that they are not out of date. The table below lists suppliers that we have found to be reliable in the past. If buying packets of seeds from a seed display, always check the condition of the packet and the "plant by" date. Also, read the description of the vegetable to ensure that you are buying what you

want. For instance, early rather than late peas and dwarf rather than climbing beans.

Good Spanish seeds can be purchased for most types of basic vegetables. However, the number of varieties available can be limited especially seeds grown organically or older varieties that have been dropped due to the cost of registering them on the approved European Community list for general commercial sale. For instance, last year we had trouble purchasing the seeds for growing "violins" or butternut squash, incidentally a wonderful squash for cooking and juicing. Our normal seed merchant was as mystified as we were but on investigation found that they had been dropped along with several other regular varieties from the catalogue. At the same time we wrote to major seed distributors in Spain to determine what organically grown seeds they sold. We found their lists short since demand was almost entirely from commercial growers of organic crops for export and only commercially viable packs and not small retail packets were sold.

Also few villagers now grow from seed but purchase mainly plantlets for convenience. When they do grow from seed it is mainly from those they have saved from the previous year's crops. Usually these are for onions, leeks, tomatoes, peppers, squashes, chard, beans, melons, sweet corn, sunflowers and potatoes. In general they buy plantlets for lettuces, cabbages, cauliflowers, globe artichokes and onions.

In addition to using Spanish seeds we therefore purchase organic seeds by mail order to achieve a greater diversity of seasonal crops and to help preserve heritage and heirloom varieties. The heritage seeds we buy are varieties once sold commercially but no longer, while heirloom seeds are seeds passed down from generation to generation, sometimes for centuries, without ever being commercially exploited.

Where possible we purchase seeds that have been sourced from a warm/hot climate.

The number of seeds in a packet varies tremendously depending on the variety, rarity of seed and supplier. However, the following are typical quantities: 10 to 20 seeds for cucumbers, squash, pumpkins and rare varieties; 50 for sweet corn, aubergines and peppers; 100 to 200 for brassicas, French beans and broad beans; 500 to 1000 for onions, radishes, rocket and broccoli; even more for carrots and lettuces. In general, the numbers supplied will match your requirements with some left over.

Normally, all or most seeds in a packet will germinate under good conditions and grow to a full-size plant. But you may experience more losses with the packets of large numbers of small seeds than with packets of only 10 large seeds.

You can also obtain seeds from neighbours, friends, and members of a local gardening club on a swap basis or even join an international seed swap network.

You can let some of your plants go to seed in order to dry, store and use them the next season and perhaps swap some. You can use some seeds for sprouting which will be much cheaper than buying packets. The easiest vegetables to collect seeds from are beans, courgettes, leeks, melons, onions, peas, peppers including Padrón peppers and hot chilli peppers, spinach, sunflowers, tomatoes and squashes of all sorts.

Two other useful sources of free seeds: from unusual vegetables that you purchase and from a particularly tasty tomato in a salad in a restaurant.

USEFUL SOURCES OF VEGETABLE SEEDS

Spanish suppliers
Packets of seeds marketed under the following names and others will be found in horticultural shops, garden shops, agricultural cooperatives, supermarkets etc. In some agricultural shops it is possible to purchase seeds such as sweet corn, peas and beans loose from large packets by weight.

Batlle, Gil Mascarell Semillas (brands include Rainbow, Hortícola, Iluns, Semillas GM, Halloween, Rocalba, Semilleros Cucala Agrícola, Semillas Falco, Semillas Fito (brands include NV Somers imported from Belgium), Carrefour. Semillas Silvestres, Córdoba, sells by mail order — their list is organic and includes many herbs, *www.semillassilvestres.com.*

Mail order imports
Companies from which you can obtain vegetable seeds by mail order include:
A. Portugal:
Germisem-sementes, a useful list of 50 organic varieties, *www.germisem.com*
B. France:
Association Kokopelli, an amazingly long, interesting list, www.kokopelli.asso.fr
Vilmorin, excellent photographs, *www.oxalis.com*
C. Ireland:
Heritage Gardening, a small but interesting international list, *www.wildaboutveg.com*
D. United Kingdom:
Agroforestry Research Trust, some unusual seeds, *www.agroforestry.co.uk*
Chiltern Seeds, an interesting list, some unusual vegetables and herbs, *www.chilternseeds.co.uk*
Mr Fothergills Seeds, a good range, *www.mr-fithergills.co.uk*
The Heritage Seed Library, selected annual list for members of seeds no longer available commercially, *enquiry@hdra.org.uk*
Jekka's Herb Farm, unusual varieties and cultivars of herbs, *www.jekkasherbfarm.com*
W. Robinson & Sons, seeds for giants!, *www.mammothonion.co.uk*
Edwin Tucker, fairly extensive interesting list, *www.tuckersmaltings.co.uk*
Sutton Seeds, excellent catalogue which indicates vitamin contents of vegetables and has selection of mini vegetables, *www.suttons-seeds.co.uk*
The Organic Gardening Catalogue, a joint venture with HDRA, good list, *www.organiccatalog.com*
Tamar Organics, some interesting varieties, *www.tamaorganics.co.uk*
Thompson and Morgan, always worth looking at, some organic seeds, *www.thompson-morgan.com*
Victoriana Nursery Gardens, very interesting list, including old varieties, *www.victoriana.ws*

b. Avoid using out-of-date seeds

It is preferable to use fresh seeds as, once a packet is open, their ability to germinate successfully tends to decrease. Some seeds even deteriorate within packets within a year and self-kept seeds within a matter of months unless correctly stored.

If you allow some plants to go to seed each year in order to keep your own seeds for the

next year, recognise that some hybrid varieties will not reproduce well. This is part of the problem with GM seeds and terminator aeeds which will not reproduce at all. By using heirloom seeds of old unmodified varieties you will have less of a problem.

c. Storage of seeds

If seeds are left over, squeeze as much air out of the packet as you can, fold over the top and seal with cellotape. Then keep in a sealed container in the fridge. If you keep your own seeds, dry them in the sun and then store in airtight containers and again keep in the fridge. Bean and pea seeds are vulnerable to weevil attacks so place in the deep freeze for three or four days to kill off any maggots or eggs before storing in the fridge.

If you keep some of your own seeds, do wash them clean of any vegetable flesh before drying them in the sun and ensure that they are fully dry before storing in airtight containers. Do not vacuum-pack them as seeds are living organisms and need oxygen to survive.

d. Use of appropriate containers

The table below illustrates the type of containers we use for raising plantlets from seed. The container chosen according to the size of the seed and the space and depth required to produce strong root balls before planting out.

TYPES OF CONTAINERS USED FOR DIFFERENT SEED

Container	Seeds	Sown	Seeds per pot or module	Why grown in containers
Pots in propagator followed by pricking out into 3cm modular tray*	Tomatoes Peppers Aubergines	February	20/30	To achieve continuously warm germination temperatures and have plants ready for planting out in May when air and soil temperatures will have warmed up
10cm pots, or peat pots, initially, in propagator	Water melons Cucumbers	March	3/5	As above
10cm pots or peat pots	Melons Pumpkins Squash	February/ March	2/3	To have plants with good root systems ready for planting out in May/June
10cm pots	Lettuces	August/ April	20/30	To have a continuity of plantlets and to protect seedlings from snails and slugs
15cm pots	Leeks Onions	August/ Winter/ Spring	30/40	Since these are slow to germinate weeds can take over if sown in the open ground and are difficult to remove without disturbing seedlings
As above then prick out into 2.5/3cm diam. 7/8cm deep modules	Broccoli Cauliflower Cabagge	July/ August	10/20	Can protect seedlings from hot summer sun. Plantlets can be grown in the modules until the weather has cooled off in early autumn
Newspaper tubes 4cm diameter 10 cm high sat in a polystyrene fish box**	Peas Broad beans	Autumn	2	We only do this if autumn rains result in the ground being too wet to prepare seedbeds and plant seeds
	Early dwarf/ climbing beans	February/ March	2	To achieve higher germination rates and an earlier crop than from sowing outside, and to infill gaps
Newspaper tubes 3cm diameter 7cm high sat in a polystyrene fish box**or other tray	Carrots Parsnips Fennel	January/ February		Outside germination and growth is possible but slow in the winter months so growing indoors and transplanting can achieve a follow on crop to those sown in the open in the autumn
Modular tray sat in polystyrene fish box or a larger tray	Sunflowers Globe Artichoke	March	2	To have early plants and protectionfrom slugs and snails

Notes:
* Both polystyrene and plastic modular trays can be used.
** The preparation and use of newspaper tubes is illustrated on page 126. First, take four pages from a newspaper and cut 23/25cm-long strips as wide as the height of the required finished tubes. Second, roll the four layers of paper into tubes of the required diameter and secure with Sellotape. Third, sit the tubes in a fish box on top of a 3cm layer of compost, placing some compost between each tube. At the same time fill the tubes with compost, plant the seeds and then cover completely so that the newspaper does not dry out. The tubes should not sit higher than the box

If you are short of spare plant pots, we suggest you use milk and juice cartons with the tops cut off as a substitute for plastic pots. Or use 5-litre water bottles with the tops cut off to leave a 10cm base. The top can be used as a cover to create a mini greenhouse. We find this useful if we have no space left in the greenhouse or cold frame when starting off seeds of salad leaf crops.

e. A good seed compost

Seeds need a light, aerated, moisture-retaining, low-nutrient content compost which is preferably soil-less. The easiest ways of providing for this are as follows:

• Buy a bag of vermiculite. This is especially useful when sowing small seeds such as peppers and tomatoes which are especially prone to damping off (rotting away at the base due to surface fungi). The seedlings of such vegetables are transplanted into modular trays when they have formed the first two leaves.

• Buy a bag of special seed compost from a garden centre that can be used for all seeds.

• As we find it quite difficult to find a good seed compost in Spain, we make up our own as follows:

Mix A: 2 parts sterilised garden compost, 1 part sharp sand to ensure good drainage, 1 part peat substitute to improve moisture retention and 1 part vermiculite to lighten, aerate and also prevent the mix from drying out. A compost/seaweed mix from an Ecopark can be used as a substitute for the garden compost and vermiculite.

Before mixing the above sieve the garden compost to remove any lumps and twigs etc. and sterilise by placing on an oven tray and heating to 100/150 degrees C for 30 minutes. Allow it to cool before adding to the other ingredients. Alternatively, put some compost inside a roasting bag and heat in a microwave oven. But you must puncture the bag before placing in the microwave otherwise it could explode. Also wet the peat substitute before adding to the dry ingredients. Then mix all the ingredients well and add water if necessary to achieve a just-damp mix. This compost can be used in all containers including modular trays when transplanting small seedlings.

Mix B: We use this in modular trays when transplanting small seedlings and when sowing larger seeds such as courgettes, pumpkins, melons and beans. The mix is 1 part compost including composted seaweed from an Ecopark composter and 1 part vermiculite or 1 part purchased peat substitute. The composted seaweed contains sufficient sand.

f. Sowing of seeds

Fill your chosen containers with dampened compost and then press down lightly to avoid air pockets. The various sizes of seeds can then be sown as follows.

• Small seeds such as lettuce, broccoli and tomatoes are best thinly sprinkled on the surface and then covered with a thin layer of vermiculite or seed compost which is then firmed down gently.

• Medium-size seeds such as onions and leeks are sown as above but with a centimetre covering of vermiculite or seed compost.

• Larger seeds such as melons, courgettes and squash are pressed down 1.5 centimetres into the compost. Push the seeds into the compost on their edge to ensure that the flat sides of the seed are not lying on wet compost and rotting.

• Peas and beans are also pressed down about 1.5 centimetres into the compost. It is useful to pre-germinate the seeds by wrapping in a damp cloth for a few days until they sprout. During this process they should be kept in the dark and the cloth kept damp.

Immediately after sowing the seeds spray the surface of the growing medium with a fungicide to reduce the chance of the damping off of emergent seedlings. It's best to use a fine hand spray for this purpose.

In cold weather the germination of seeds can be accelerated by:

• placing pots or trays in a propagator

• covering pots or trays with a sheet of glass and placing in direct sunlight

• placing the pots or trays in a heated greenhouse or sunny cold frame, or

• covering the pots or trays with a clear plastic bag raised up above the soil with a simple wire frame and then sealed. The sealing prevents moisture loss but one needs to be vigilant that the conditions are not so wet that damping off occurs, or too hot due to being too much in the sun. Remove glass and plastic covers as soon as the seedlings are half a centimetre high. Uncovered pots and trays need to be checked daily to ensure that they are still moist and if not water lightly

g. Timely sowing

The best time to plant different types of seeds depends on:

• The germination temperature required. For instance, lettuces and carrots will germinate at as low as 12 degrees C but pumpkin need a minimum of around 20 degrees. In practice most vegetables germinate between 12 and 24 degrees although the optimums may be slightly higher and the time required for the seed to actually germinate in the soil are generally between five and 14 days. Radishes requiring less than a week are among the quickest and parsley and parsnips requiring up to three weeks are among the slowest.

In practice the above temperatures are not that difficult to achieve either in spring or autumn which in Spain is, for vegetable growers, a second spring. However, there is often confusion about the germination temperature given in seed catalogues and on packets. They may refer to the minimum temperature required for germination, or in other cases to the optimum temperature which can be twice as high as illustrated in the diagram below.

The temperatures are not the air temperatures but the soil temperatures required at the depth of the seeds and some seeds need to be sown at only half a centimetre below the surface and others at five to 10. Further, when you go to sow some seeds on an April day, it can be 20 degrees in the shade but the air temperature in the sun — which is what heats up the soil — can be up to 50 degrees. At other times the temperature could be the same in a glassed-in area as it is on your vegetable plot. No wonder many gardeners, as well as the seeds, get very confused about what is going on.

• The time from germination to first harvests. This can vary from just a few weeks for cut-

and-come-again lamb's lettuce crops and radishes to six months for pumpkins and squashes.

• The latest that you can expect to harvest crops. For instance late climbing beans can be sown for autumn harvesting but this will need to be done not later than mid-July.

• Whether you want to provide for continuity of crops by raising and planting several successive batches of vegetables such as lettuces, beans and brassicas, carrots, radishes and potatoes.

• The low frost resistance of the seedlings such as tomatoes and peppers.

• The facilities you have for maintaining above ambient temperatures to raise early seeds.

• The low heat resistance of some seedlings such as lettuces. However it is important to sow brassicas such as broccoli, cabbages and cauliflowers in July in order to have plantlets to plant out in the autumn.

h. Labelling

Make your labels before starting to sow your seeds as there is nothing worse than forgetting what is in each pot or tray. You can buy plastic markers with either special marker pens or pencils. We prefer the latter as the writing doesn't fade so fast in the hot Spanish sun.

In recent years we have made our own labels by typing in bold type a list of seeds with their dates of planting on the computer. The list is then printed off and cut into strip labels. Each is then sealed in cellotape to make them waterproof and a small length of wire pushed through the label and attached to a short stick. Each label can then be pushed into the soil of each pot or tray as soon as the seeds are sown. This form of label has the advantage that it can be transferred to the top of a cane to label the plantlets when they are planted out on the vegetable plot. Ensure you use tall canes when you plant out peas or beans so that you can still see the labels when the plants grow up.

Preparing labels this way also means that you have an up-to-date list of sowings saved on your computer._

i. Recognising and solving problems quickly

Seeds generally fail to germinate for the following reasons:

• Seeds are out of date or have not been stored well.

• Growing medium allowed to dry out or is made too wet.

• The pots and trays are in a too-cool or too-shady situation.

If you have failures, sow another batch of fresh seeds in fresh pots and soil in case there were fungal spores in the soil.

Similarly, the reasons young seedlings don't develop well are:

• Insufficient moisture.

• Temperature too low.

• Too much shade.

• They have reached a point where they have used up the initial store of nutrients contained in the seeds. In this case it is time to start feeding with a dilute nitrogen feed.

• Too much moisture and you forget to spray the surface with a fungicide when sowing the seeds and when seedlings emerge. So they rot. If this starts to happen, quickly remove the unhealthy seedlings and dry the compost until it is just damp to touch. Then lightly spray the remaining seedlings and soil with a dilute fungicide mix. We use a natural herbal horsetail infusion but proprietary fungicides are also available.

j. Careful transplanting of seedlings

As already indicated, many seedlings will need transplanting into larger pots or modular trays. First fill the pots or trays with the compost prepared as in d above and then dampen with a very dilute liquid fertiliser. Either use a proprietary general fertiliser, liquid seaweed feed or a nettle/comfrey feed prepared as in Section 5.3. Then prick out the seedlings individually when they have two leaves, holding them by their leaves and never by their fragile stems. Make a planting hole the depth of the roots of the seedling with a pencil or similar diameter stick, lower the roots gently into the hole, and then carefully fill in the hole. Finally, lightly firm the compost around the stem of the seedling. Don't disregard any smaller seedlings as sometimes they grow on to be the strongest plantlets.

Seedlings can rot very easily at this stage if over-watered so don't water again until they are just starting to dry out. From then on feed once a week with a weak solution of one of the aforesaid liquid fertilisers to encourage strong healthy growth.

Place the pots and trays of transplants in a greenhouse or cold frame until the weather is warm enough to harden them off in the open air before finally planting them out.

To ensure that plantlets are not eaten by slugs or snails always keep several bran or beer traps in the greenhouse or cold frame or as a last resort sprinkle some slug pellets around.

k. Light and temperature control

Once seeds germinate, the containers need to be kept in a light warm situation to sustain their growth and to prevent them from getting unduly leggy. This is no problem once the danger of frosts is past but before then you will need to resort to one of the following: a shelf in a heated green house, a sunny windowsill, a tabletop inside a window or the door on to a south-facing terrace not used during the winter (we use our study once the greenhouse is full with over-wintering delicate flowering plants).

Larger seeds such as beans, squashes, courgettes and pumpkins can be sown in pots in late February/early March and placed in a double-skinned plastic sheet cold frame (soon knocked up from a few scraps of wood) or a proprietary cold frame placed in a sunny position.

Since young seedlings have a tendency to grow towards the light, it is wise to turn pots and trays 180 degrees around every couple of days.

If you need to heat a greenhouse, this can best be done with a small, thermostatically controlled, electric, sealed oil-filled radiator or with a solar heating system.

When temperatures warm up, it may be necessary to shade your greenhouse and cold frame. We use a lightweight woven plastic sheet that although it shades does give some light and does not rot if it gets wet.

If growing seeds on a windowsill, it may be necessary to move them back away from the glass during the hottest part of the day.

l. Moisture control

Ensure that the sowing compost is just damp before you sow the seeds and then test the compost daily. If it starts to dry out, dampen with a fine rose watering can, fine sprayer or a 1.5-litre water bottle with a screw-on fine rose head. These have started to appear in garden centres or can be obtained from Thompson & Morgan by mail order. See Section 4.12 for the address.

m. Feeding of plantlets

Most plantlets will benefit from a weekly dilute, general, organic balanced feed. Many such products are now available or you can use a dilute homemade feed as outlined in Section 5.3.

n. Hardening off

Plantlets raised under cover will need to be acclimatised in a sheltered corner of the garden for a few days before being planted out in their final position. Check that the temperatures are not forecast to drop dramatically before doing so. It is a good idea to bring in the plantlets at night for the first two days. Also ensure that you place them where they will not be damaged by heavy unexpected rain or rainwater running off an unguttered roof.

o. Timely and careful planting out

Having raised strong healthy plants, do ensure that you get them off to a good start when planted out in your containers, raised beds or vegetable plot. We suggest the following good practice:

- Prepare the soil in advance — see Section 4.3.
- Decide whether to plant through holes in black plastic or just into the soil. The advantages of black plastic are that it inhibits weed growth and reduces moisture loss through evaporation.

Plants typically planted through plastic are tomatoes, peppers, cucumbers, courgettes, aubergines and sometimes onions. Squashes, pumpkins and melons are best not planted through plastic as they need to put down air roots along their stems to extract the extra moisture and nutrients necessary for large fruits.

- Do not plant out any plantlets until they have good root structure and are strong enough to withstand wind and rain.
- Plant out if possible on a good day according to the lunar calendar — see Section 4.15.
- Water pots or trays of plantlets shortly before attempting to remove them.
- Remove plantlets carefully from their pots by knocking the pot and lifting out the entire compost and root ball/s in one piece if possible. If there are several plantlets in the pot, separate them carefully retaining as much compost as possible around each root ball when dividing them. When removing from modular trays, check whether you can merely lift each plantlet out easily. If not, use the handle of an old teaspoon or a plastic plant label to loosen them.
- Prepare appropriate-sized planting holes with a trowel or dibber (round-ended piece of wood or stick). Then plant carefully avoiding damage to roots stems and leaves. Firm the soil around the plantlets, ensuring in most cases that they are not planted any deeper than they were in the pots or trays.

The important exceptions are as follows:

- Onions should be planted so that their roots are 3cm deep.
- Leeks are best planted 5–8cm deep depending on the size of plantlet, leaving not less than 4cm of green leaf above the soil. The deeper they are the more blanched they become and they are best watered in rather than physically filling the holes with soil.
- The top third of the green leaves of onions and leeks should be cut off before planting to encourage root rather than leaf growth.

• Leggy tomato plants can be planted up to half their depth by digging a deeper planting hole or planting shallowly and horizontally.

• If plantlets have long stringy roots, trim them to encourage stronger root balls.

• Similarly, elongated stems of peppers and brassicas can be planted more deeply.

• Melons, squash, pumpkins and cucumbers are best planted on low mounds above pre-prepared holes (30-50cm diameter and 40-50cm deep) filled with a compost/manure/soil mix.

• Plant and firm soil and then construct a moat around the plants for effective watering. To ensure the soil around the stem is not washed away, construct a cone of soil around the stem as illustrated.. Water all plantlets once planted.

• Slugs and snails love many young plants so protect them immediately. A circle of slug bait can be used, but we prefer to use non-chemical methods (see Section 5.7).

p. Protection of early plantings

Plantlets planted before air temperatures have warmed up and especially if there is still any danger of night frosts should be protected by covering them with cloches. See Section 5.1.

4.13 GROWING VEGETABLES FROM SEEDS IN OPEN GROUND

Success factors for sowing seeds directly into the ground on a raised bed, vegetable plot or larger allotment:

a. Selection, freshness and storage of seeds.

b. Preparation of soil appropriate to type of seed.

c. Temperature of soil.

d. Control of weeds.

e. Timing of plantings.

f. Moisture content of soil.

g. Planting depths and spacings.

h. Reap the benefits of companion plantings.

i. Avoiding close planting of incompatible plants.

j. Protection against extreme weather.

k. Careful watering.

l. Attraction of beneficial insects and animals.

m. Disease and pest prevention and control.

We consider each in the sections that follow.

a. Selection, freshness and storage of seeds

This has already been dealt with in detail in Section 4.12.

b. Preparation of soil appropriate to type of seed

Although the initial improvement of your soil will have produced a healthy and fertile soil, some vegetables grow best if the areas where they are to be planted are further enriched as already indicated in Sections 4.5 to 4.8. The main requirements are:

• Potatoes are best planted in trenches lined with a layer of well-rotted compost/manure and comfrey leaves if you have them and then earthed up.

• Beans are best planted over a trench previously filled with compost, manure and kitchen vegetable waste (that need not have been rotted down previously) and then covered with 7/8cm of soil.

• Pumpkins, squashes, courgettes and melons are best planted above 30/40cm deep, 40 cm circumference holes filled with well-rotted compost/manure the previous winter and then covered with 7/8cm of soil.

• Peas benefit from raking in 2cm of well-rotted compost into the surface of the seed bed.

• Small seeds such as lettuce, carrots, parsnips, fennel, onions and leeks need a fine seedbed prepared by raking the top 4cm of soil to a fine tilth and removing any lumps of earth or stones.

c. Temperature of soil

As discussed in Section 4.12, the soil temperatures at which vegetable seeds germinate can vary considerably. If you are planting early crops, it is important to allow the soil to warm up on sunny days. If the weather is cold, you can accelerate the warming by covering seed beds with plastic cloches, sheets of black plastic or an old carpet.

d. Control of weeds

The worst thing is a seed bed in which weed seeds germinate and grow quicker and more vigorously than the vegetable seeds you have sown. It is therefore worth doing what you can to minimise the problem before you plant your seeds.

First, keep any unplanted ground and planted ground as weed-free as you can, bearing in mind what we say in Section 5.6 about not being too finicky in wanting a totally tidy plot especially if you garden organically.

Second, it is helpful to cover any unplanted areas as in c above and then uncover. Weed seeds will germinate within a few days. Leave them to grow for a week and then either remove by hand or kill off with a flame or infrared wand before sowing your seeds. Unfortunately, the use of the latter two will probably kill off some beneficial worms and organisms. This will also occur if you use weed-killers which would also require that you delay the planting of seeds until any residual effects have disappeared.

e. Timing of plantings

This topic has been fully covered in Sections 4.5 to 4.8 for individual types of vegetables.

f. Moisture content of soil

Ideally seed beds and the soil around the stems and down to the lower extremities of the root balls of emergent plants will be kept just damp day in, day out. This is easily achieved with timer-controlled piped watering systems but less so when using Moorish-style flooding of seed and growing beds (discussed in more detail in Section 4.16).

g. Planting depths and spacings

The depth of the soil over seeds can have a detrimental or beneficial impact on germination and growth.

If seeds are covered with too little soil, there will be insufficient moisture in the upper layer of the soil to stimulate and sustain germination when seed beds dry out between waterings.

If seeds are sown too deeply, they will not become warm enough as the thick layer above will act as an insulator and prevent the heat of the sun's rays from penetrating below the first centimetre or so of soil. Typical depths have already been suggested in Section 4.12.

To ensure that all plants receive the maximum benefit from the sun's rays, plant rows or oblong blocks on a north-south axis. There is evidence that the earth's magnetic field is of benefit to avoid planting along geophysical lines.

Re spacing, we suggest that you plant closer than traditionally in the UK and Spain in order to control weeds and minimise the evaporation of moisture from the soil. Typical spacings are indicated in the table below.

Type of seeds	Suggested spacing of seeds (cm)	Traditional spacing of seeds (cm)	Suggested planting depths (cm)	Nº of seeds per sowing hole or sprinkled*	Spacing when planted on as plantiets or thinned (cm)
Asparagus**	5	5	3/4	2	60/90
Beetroot****	5	5	2/3	2	10/15
Broad beans	20	40/50*	4/5	4/5	20
Broccoli**	5	5	2/3	2/3	40/50
Cabbages**	5	5	2/3	2/3	30/40
Carrots***	Sprinkle thinly	Sprinkle	1/2	Sprinkle	2/3
Climbing beans	15/20	25/30	4/5	3	15/20
French beans	10/15	20/25	4/5	3	10/15
Fennel****	5	20/25	1/2	3	15/20
Leeks**	Sprinkle thinly	Sprinkle	1	Sprinkle	10
Lettuces**	Sprinkle thinly	Sprinkle	0,5	Sprinkle	15/20
Melons***	150/200	300/400	4/5	4/5	150/200
Onions**	Sprinkle thinly	Sprinkle	1	Sprinkle	10
Parsnips***	10	10	1/2	3	10
Peas	10	15/20	4/5	4/5	10
Courgettes***	100/150	200/250	4/5	2/3	100/150
Squash***	150/300	300/400	3/4	2/3	150/200
Sweet corn****	15/20	30/40	4/5	2	15/20

* Small seeds can be sprinkled in drills (a long shallow trench) or scattered over square seed beds.
** These vegetables are normally grown in seed beds and then transplanted to permanent growing beds when the plantlets have formed a good root systems.
*** These vegetables are grown to maturity in the bed in which they are sown but they will normally need careful thinning to allow the remaining plants the space to grow healthily to maturity.
****Some of the stronger thinnings can be planted on as if grown for plantlets and many can be eaten young in salads.
e.g., parsnips, fennel and beetroot. We have had some success with carrots when thinned and planted on in conveniently wet weather.

h. Reap the benefits of companion plantings

There are considerable benefits in planting certain plants adjacent to each other as illustrated below:

• A sturdy plant can provide the support for another vegetable that is a climber, e.g. climbing beans grow well up sweet corn which is sown two weeks before the beans.

There is also another symbiotic relationship, i.e. mutually beneficial relationship between the two plants. The roots of beans build up nitrogen in the soil and sweet corn is a nitrogen addict.

• Some plants are beneficial in repelling pests that attack other vegetables, e.g. onions and garlic planted around rows or blocks of carrots can minimise the possibility of carrot fly attacks. A similar effect can be achieved by burying the tops cut off onion plantlets before planting or of cut up chives in the seed bed.

• Other plants are beneficial in attracting pests off affected plants, e.g. nasturtiums and marigolds can attract black fly away from broad beans and spinach. Similarly, marigolds planted between cucumbers, squashes and melons can reduce the incidence of beetle attacks; tomatoes grown among asparagus can keep away the asparagus beetle; mint in a buried pot can deter ants, aphids and cabbage butterflies; fennel and coriander allowed to go to seed around the edge of the vegetable plot attract beetles that might otherwise attack the vegetables. Several other herbs are useful in this way including oregano, rosemary, sage, chives and borage. Within the herb garden rosemary and sage can protect the more delicate basil from insects.

• A row of chrysanthemum plants can attract beneficial insects as well as making the vegetable garden colourful.

• Rows of well-supported tall plants like climbing beans, sunflowers and sweet peas

are useful as wind and sun breaks to protect more delicate plants.

• Sunflowers, sweet peas, borage and roses, traditional on many Spanish vegetable plots, are excellent for attracting pollinators for fruiting vegetable plants such as peas, beans, tomatoes, peppers, aubergines, squashes, melons, cucumbers and courgettes.

• Comfrey is a good deterrent to snails and slugs. We use it in three ways in this respect: 1. Leaves placed around young melon and squash plants etc. 2. By placing a layer of leaves under potatoes when planting in either holes or trenches. 3. We split some of our comfrey plants annually so that we now have a continuous barrier around the circumference of our large vegetable plot.

By following the above principles your vege-table plot may start to look a little like an old cottage garden but that was why mixed flower and vegetable beds were not only colourful and productive but often largely plague-free.

i. Avoiding close planting of incompatible plants

Some plants have an antagonistic and negative influence on other plants. For instance, beans and peas dislike being near onions and leeks and vice versa; tomatoes are better grown away from peppers, aubergine, fennel and sweet corn; courgettes, squashes and melons are best grown away from potatoes although all these crops like plenty of manure in the soil. Ensure that your crop rotation plan (see Section 5.7) recognises these potential problems.

j. Protection against extreme weather

See Section 5.1.

k. Careful watering

We find that we produce the tastiest, crispiest and healthiest vegetables by watering just sufficiently to sustain normal growth and not by constant over-watering that can tend to produce watery and less appetising vegetables especially with crops such as lettuces, tomatoes and melons. Watering is fully discussed in Section 4.16.

l. Attraction and retention of beneficial insects and animals

The attraction of beneficial insects by companion planting has already been discussed in 'i' above. However it is important not to use chemical insecticides, pesticides, fungicides and weed killers if you want to reap the maximum benefit of their presence.

It is also advantageous to attract and retain the presence of frogs, toads, lizards and hedgehogs that can feed on insects and slugs.

We found that within three years we had a balanced eco system that required only the occasional need to spray against the invasion of insects and on those occasions we have

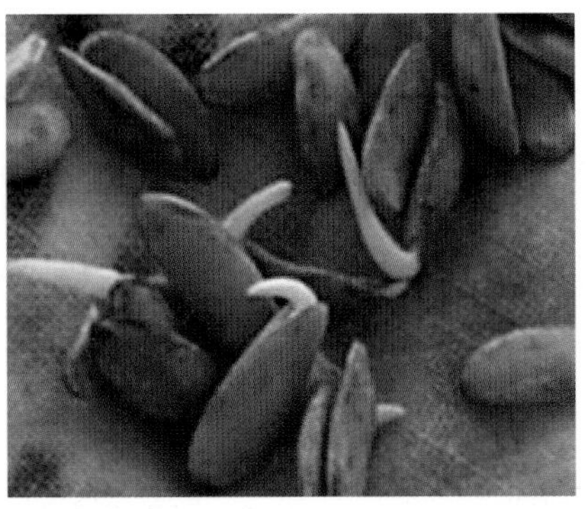

only used naturally/ecologically controls. These are described in section 5.7. To attract the above animals it is worthwhile placing a small pond, a pile of rocks, a stack of logs, and a loose pile of garden rubbish on the edge of the vegetable plot.

m. Disease and pest prevention and control

Biological/ecological/organic proprietary products are available for all the insects, pests and plague problems you are likely to meet. Look for them in your local horticultural shops, garden centres and agricultural cooperatives rather than using more hazardous chemical products which often require protective clothing. If you can't find things locally, the Organic Gardening Catalogue (www.organiccatalogue.com) is a useful source of products by mail order but in most cases they would need to be delivered to a UK address.

There are many easily prepared home-made insect and pest deterrents and controls, as described in Section 5.7.

4.14 GROWING FROM BULBS

The following vegetables can be grown from various types of bulbs:

Onions, shallots from sets or bulbs as an alternative to growing from seed or buying plantlets. However, the availability in Spain is not that reliable and the number of varieties available is limited. However, if you see a packet, it is certainly worth having a go.

Garlic by planting the individual cloves. These can be obtained by dividing any garlic corm you buy as you would for cooking. Occasionally you will find specially selected large crowns available for sale in horticultural shops or agricultural cooperatives.

Jerusalem artichokes by planting small rhizomes. Look around for these in specialist greengrocers. They are available in several UK catalogues.

Ginger and turmeric are also grown from small rhizomes. Again watch out for fresh rhizomes in supermarkets and specialist greengrocers.

Saffron, an autumn crocus, is invaluable for colouring and flavouring fish and meat dishes — saffron-flavoured pineapple is one of our favourite healthy desserts.

Tips for growing from bulbs are given in section 4.5.

4.15 USING A LUNAR CALENDAR

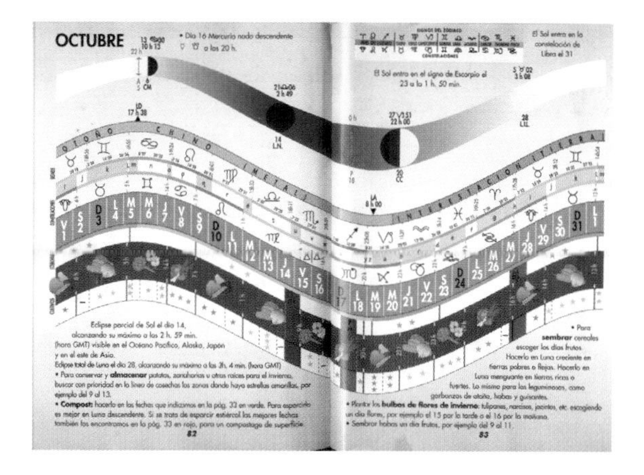

Many Spaniards still remember sitting outside after dark being instructed by their elders on the basics of astronomy and the impact of the cyclic positions of the moon, planets, constellations and the sun in relation to the earth and each other and the best timings for the planting of vegetables and fruits, the healthy growing of the plants and the quality of their harvests.

Hearing these tales, we purchased our first lunar calendar, became fascinated and tried to do likewise when we had a quiet summer evening. Unfortunately, our studies were foreshortened when street lights were installed which prevent us seeing the total night skyscape.

But the Spaniards were not the first to garden this way. Historians tell us that the Egyptians, Chinese, Celts, Greeks, Romans, Arabs and American Indians all followed a form of astronomic calendar and agriculturalists and scholarly monks continued its development in medieval Europe. Parts of the knowledge were passed down generation to generation in agricultural communities and favourite days became established for planting various vegetables, such as the rule that you should plant potatoes by St. Patrick's Day, broad beans on All Saints day (November 1) and paella beans a few days either side of St. James's Day (July 25). Interestingly, this is not just folklore. The lunar calendar for 2006 matched St. Patrick's Day exactly and is never more than a day or two adrift.

Rudolf Steiner, an Austrian, collated what was known, carried out his own research, and in 1924 published his concept of the lunar/solar calendar and its practical application. Research has continued and more and more farmers and gardeners are adopting his concepts of the lunar calendar and "biodynamic gardening" — responding to the ever-changing but cyclic cosmic rhythms of the universe.

Today's published agricultural/gardening calendars incorporate and interpret how all the known cause-effect relationships within the lunar solar universe (such as the impacts on the earth's electromagnetic field, temperatures, rainfalls, tides, length of night and day, gravity pulls, sun flare activity etc.) affect humans, animals, insects, birds and plants. Luckily the end result is presented in a form easily understood by layman gardeners like ourselves.

The chart above is an extract from the lunar calendar we use. It is published annually in Spain by Artus Porta Manresa. We find it the easiest to follow of all the calendars we have seen and also the most comprehensive. It is normally available from November onwards in bookshops. If you have difficulties in tracing it, contact calendario@lunar.infomail.es.

There is a page similar to the one illustrated for each month of the year. One does not need to be an astrologer or understand much Spanish to use it, as everything for the amateur gardener is in the bottom two lines of the diagram above.

The four groups of vegetables root, fruit, leaf and flower are very obviously illustrated. The best days for doing any work on each of the groups of vegetables is indicated by three stars, the second-best days by two stars and the also-rans by one star. Days when no work should be done are indicated by the red boxes.

So, for example, in the month illustrated the best days for work related to fruit vegetables were the 19th and 20th, for leaf vegetables the eighth and 25th, for root crops the 13th, thirtieth and 31st and for flower vegetables the 23rd and 24th. For the amateur gardener, the most important aspects are that they sow seeds, plant plantlets, give extra feeds, and harvest vegetables for storing on the three or two-star days.

By the way, the wave curve of the charts indicates when the moon is rising and falling in the night sky. The clear and shaded moons on the top curve indicate the pattern of the waxing and waning moon. The lines below relate to the relationships between the planets and constellations and the moon, which are for the astrological scholars.

Biodynamic agriculturalists following the vegetable-growing practices first expounded by George Steiner aim to do all the work on fields and greenhouses of specific groups of vegetables (root, leaf, flower and fruit) including all the tasks mentioned above (plus ploughing, hoeing, harrowing, weeding, watering, pruning extra growth and flowers etc.) on the most beneficial days according to the lunar/solar calendar.

Biodynamic farming is a growing phenomenon worldwide. We go as far as is practical, bearing in mind that we don't work on the vegetable plot all day/every day, and that it would be extremely difficult to do so with a mixed plot of up to 50 types of vegetables compared with a commercial mono-crop field and taking into account rainy days and holidays.

The calendar is also packed with other useful easy-to-read charts. The information of most interest to the practical gardener includes when to cut canes, when to plant and prune fruit trees, when to spray against insects and fungi, when to best have your hair cut, etc.

4.16 WATERING YOUR VEGETABLES EFFECTIVELY

How, when and how much you water your vegetables, whether in pots, raised beds or a vegetable plot, will have a major impact on their survival, speed of growth and quality and also on your watering bill. The quality of the water you use can also have an impact.

HOW AND WHEN TO WATER

There are four main methods.

1. With a watering can or fine spray hose for vegetables planted in pots, tubs, and small raised beds. Water on a regular basis to keep the surface of the soil just damp and the plants growing at a steady rate. As the plants grow you will need to increase the amount of water accordingly, especially for fruiting vegetables such as tomatoes when the fruits are forming and swelling. In very hot weather you may need to water small seedlings daily, even early morning and late evening.

2. With a drip irrigation system fitted with a timer so that watering times and durations can be set. Such systems are not difficult to put together and can be used to water a collection of pots and raised beds as well as a fully fledged vegetable plot. The necessary plastic tubing, joints, sprays and hole-piercing tools are available in many garden centres, horticultural shops and agricultural cooperatives and, in the main vegetable and fruit-growing areas, from dedicated irrigation system shops or warehouses.

A – Laying out a drip/woven tube irrigation system

B – A useful kit for a small system

Photograph 'A' illustrates how to layout a basic system. Photograph 'B' shows the contents of a very useful kit marketed by Hozelock which includes all the tubing, fittings, spray and drip heads and the battery-operated timer you need for an efficient small-scale system. This can be very convenient when you only have a small area to water and you are not a handyman.

3. Perforated, porous and woven plastic tubes are practical alternatives to a drip system. The perforated tubes are best for watering plants with a gap of 10, 20 and 30 centimetres or more between them. Woven tubes can be rigid or go flat when not operating . They wet a continuous strip of soil as opposed to only beneath each drip head. They are therefore particularly useful for watering rows of closely planted vegetables.

4. If you water by flooding from irrigation channels during the late autumn and winter, it is preferable to water in the morning to ensure that any surface moisture has drained away and any watered plants are dry before the chance of overnight air frosts.

During the rest of the year we prefer to water in the evening when the sun is dropping and the temperatures are lower. In this way most water soaks down into the ground, there are minimum evaporation losses and less chance of the surface of saturated soil drying to an impervious hard-baked cake.

HOW MUCH TO WATER

The amount of water you use depends on:

a. The type of crops planted. For instance, tomatoes are very thirsty plants while melons need little watering once planted. The thirstiness of various types of vegetables is discussed in more detail in Sections 4.5 to 4.8.

b. The density of crops. The more crops planted the more water required and the more space between plants the less shading of the surface of the soil and the greater the evaporation losses.

a. The maturity of the plants. Just-emerged seeds with very shallow roots will need frequent watering to wet the soil to a depth of three or four centimetres. This will need to be increased as the roots develop and go deeper. Maturing plants will require a good soak to get down to the lowest roots.

b. The water-retaining capacity of your soil. The more organic matter you work into the soil the greater the capacity to retain water, reduce evaporation and drainage losses. The need for watering is therefore reduced.

c.Hoeing and harrowing bare areas of soil reduces losses and subsequently reduces the amount of watering required.

d. Variations in the pressure of the feed to your watering system. It's preferable to fit a water pressure regulator.

e. Whether you plant through holes in plastic sheeting. This obviously reduces evaporation losses considerably and can be used in conjunction with a drip system run under or over the plastic sheeting as well as when watering by flooding.

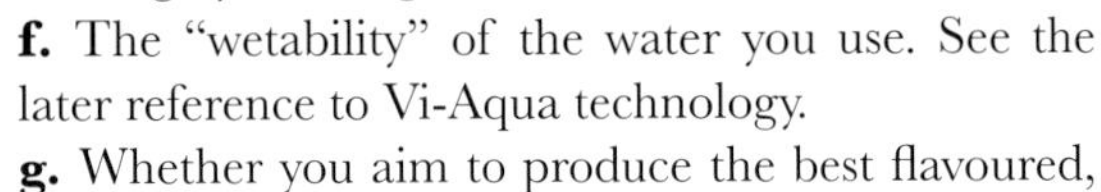

f. The "wetability" of the water you use. See the later reference to Vi-Aqua technology.

g. Whether you aim to produce the best flavoured, textured and coloured vegetables or are attempting to grow the biggest.

Since we grow to maximise the pleasure and healthiness of our meals, we aim for the former — except when watering a couple of pumpkin plants as we would still like to beat the 100-kilo barrier.

When you grow your own vegetables you will soon notice the difference between, for instance, onions, garlic, tomatoes and lettuces grown at a natural rate to maximise the concentration of taste, oils, vitamins and minerals and those forced to grow faster by watering two or three times as much.

For example, we flood most of our vegetables every seven to 10 days in the hottest weeks of the year while nearby Spaniards are watering every three days. Their vegetables grown for selling in local shops and markets as well as for family eating can be rather tasteless, over-fleshy and in any case are far too big for a small household wanting to harvest fresh vegetables daily with the minimum waste.

We have measured the amount of water we use by flooding and also the amount a neighbour uses with a drip irrigation system during the driest summer weeks when both our plots are fully planted and plants are maturing. We use around 30 litres per square metre during our weekly flooding and he 2.5 litres per square metre during his daily watering. Both very affordable, we using inexpensive agricultural water and free spring water during the winter — if we have had heavy rains — and our neighbour normal town water. As illustrated in the photograph, he fills up two 1,000-litre calibrated plastic tanks and uses 200 litres each time he waters by gravity. He can therefore control the amount of water he uses on a daily basis. Also much of the chlorine content will evaporate during the week.

IMPROVING THE QUALITY OF THE WATER YOU USE

a. Filtration

It's very beneficial to fit a coarse and fine filter on both incoming domestic or agricultural water supplies to remove the small particles that can block fine irrigating jets, fine tubing and fine watering-can roses.

b. Desalination

If you have saline water, small-scale direct-osmosis desalination units are available. Check with a major swimming pool supply shop.

c. Vi-Aqua

Vi-Aqua is a technology that has been shown to stimulate the strong healthy growth of seedling/plantlets and the final yield of vegetables. The technology energises water by using a low-frequency radio wave electromagnetic source which modifies the state of hydrogen molecules in water. The energised water has an improved wetting ability and enables roots to extract nutrients more easily from the soil. This improved extraction rate can lead to the use of less irrigation water for the same size of vegetable. Battery-operated units are available for stirring watering cans, adding to the end of hoses or fitting into the feeder pipe for an irrigation system. The units have been endorsed by the Royal Horticultural Gardens at Kew. Contact www.viaqua.ie or 00 353 872 500 181 for more information.

d. Grosse GIE

This is a technology that enlivens dead or impure water by modifying its molecular/crystal structure and oxygen content by magnetic and vortex means. The latter by a micro method that parallels the energising of water in turbulent mountain streams or in vortex systems developed within the biodynamic agricultural fraternity. This has been demonstrated to be of benefit to growers of vegetables whether using town, agricultural or contaminated well water.

The stand-alone units require no electricity. Domestic water treated with a Grosse unit has human health as well as plant health benefits. It can be an effective supplement to the eating of healthy vegetables and fruit. For more information contact www. lumenssaludnatural.com or www.agua-viva.info.

e. Reduction of soil Ph

Using stored rain water and adding composts, leaf mould, seaweed and manures can lower Ph values (see 4.3F).

f. Addition of fertilisers

If you have a pumped or gravity-fed irrigation system, you can add measured quantities of biological/organic fertilisers to the irrigation water on a daily or regular basis. This is preferable to adding chemical fertilisers but in both cases the constant overfeeding of vegetables can result in watery, fleshy pest-attracting growth.

g. Washing chlorine or salt from soil

If your vegetable growing area is contaminated accidentally by the backwash or emptying of your own or a neighbour's swimming pool, or if without your noticing it your well goes saline, you can wash the contamination out of the soil by spraying or flooding with good water. But it may take time and the amount of water and number of treatments required will obviously be determined by the extent of the original contamination and how quickly the water soaks through the subsoil taking the contamination with it.

h. Use of swimming pool water

Drought conditions can result in months-long bans on the use of hosepipes and irrigation systems attached to the domestic water supply. Some gardeners stop cleaning their swimming pools so they can use the water to save their flower gardens and enable them to still grow a few vegetables. If you are in this situation, don't use the water until tests show a zero residual chlorine content and a Ph reading below 7. Don't worry about the water going green, but do place a few goldfish and some oxygenating weed into the pool. The fish love to dine on mosquito larva that appear.

i. Recycling of domestic water

If the likelihood of restrictions increases in your area, consider the following actions to recycle clean water for watering your vegetables:

- Save water from boiling or steaming vegetables.
- Use ecological biodegradable washing powders or liquids and divert the rinse cycle of the washing machine to a holding tank from which vegetables can be watered.
- Run shower and bath water to a larger holding tank.
- If in a rural area, install an eco loo.
- Install an efficient "biodigester" plant that from household waste produces water sufficiently pure to recycle for gardening, washing the car and filling the pool.
- Mix TerraCottem soil enhancer into the soil mix prepared for all containers, into the bottom of seed drills and holes in seed beds, and into the bottom of larger sowing or planting trenches.This can reduce your irrigation needs by more than fifty percent. See www.terravida.com for more details of recent research by Murcia University.

4.17 HARVESTING, PREPARATION, STORAGE AND PROCESSING OF CROPS

A. DAILY HARVESTING

1. When possible harvest daily or even twice daily to ensure you enjoy raw or cooked vegetables at their freshest, crispiest, most tender, most flavoursome and while they retain most of their stored natural vitamins and minerals.

2. Start to harvest when vegetables first reach an edible size. Young lettuce and spinach leaves, carrots etc. are wonderful in salads as well as for cooking. Also the thinning achieved by taking out some young plants will provide more space for the remaining plants to grow to full maturity. Similarly the picking of young fruit vegetables such as string beans, broad beans, courgettes, Padrón peppers, peas and mangetout will encourage follow-on flowerings and fruits and the removal of some lettuce, chard, spinach and celery leaves will encourage new young growth. If you collect a small amount of whatever is young, perhaps even 20 varieties of vegetables, some interesting winter as well as summer salads can be prepared.

The above practices will allow you to enjoy such crops over an extended period of time compared to waiting until all the plants of a particular crop are mature and then harvesting

all at once. If harvesting for the commercial market that would make sense, but these days not many families are large enough to cope with gluts of varieties of vegetables that cannot be stored.

3. Remove inedible roots and leaves. Put the freshest aside to feed to poultry or animals, or recycle immediately to the compost heap or wormery (Section 5.5). Wash vegetables in running water and if not for immediate use store in the refrigerator.

4. Before placing in the refrigerator wrap leaf vegetables in a clean damp cloth or kitchen towel paper. Root crops such as carrots and radishes are best kept in a container of fresh water. Change water daily.

B. HARVESTING AND STORAGE FOR LATER USE

The following vegetables can be stored for later provided they are carefully harvested and stored. As mentioned, vegetables for storage are best harvested on the appropriate date on the lunar calendar, e.g. a three-star fruit day for squash and a three-star root day for potatoes (see section 4.15, Using a lunar calendar).

All vegetables harvested for storage should be first cleaned of soil, dried and stored as follows:

a. *Colgar* tomatoes — hang the entire trusses from a beam or hook in a cool, airy place.

b. Squash, pumpkins, marrows and melons on shelves or the floor of a dry cool cellar, shed or garage or on a shaded balcony. The pumpkins and squash can also be stored outside, even as natural ornaments around the garden, until used but they may not last as long as those stored under cover.

c. Potatoes, carrots and Jerusalem artichokes can be stored in peat but we find that in the dry, warm Spanish climate it is better to leave them in the ground and harvest fresh when required.

d. Onions and garlic can be hung up in bunches or in bags or when really dry stored in slatted plastic or wooden boxes.

e. Hot red peppers are best strung up on strings in the sun to dry. When the autumn rains come, they should be moved to a sheltered, dry, covered terrace or conservatory.

f. Some varieties of beans such as haricots, butter and soya can be left on the plants until the pods dry. Then harvest, pod the beans and dry further in a warm airy but shady place. Then place in the deep freeze for a day or two to kill off any weevils and store in sealed jars or plastic containers. In all cases check weekly to ensure that nothing is rotting or being eaten. If so, destroy.

C. PROCESSING OF NON-KEEPING GLUTS

Whether you plan to have excess crops for processing for non-seasonal use or it results by accident due to perfect climatic conditions, you will inevitably have gluts of such vegetables as beans, peas, courgettes, peppers and tomatoes. These can be processed by: bottling using the *baño María* (bain-marie) method still widely used in Spain; freezing; salting, drying and using in chutneys, pickles and jams.

Crops such as herbs, hot peppers, courgettes, wild mushrooms, onions and tomatoes can be dried during their main growing seasons for non-seasonal use. Herbs are best hung in bunches in the shade of a south-facing covered terrace or conservatory rather than in full sun to minimise the loss of the natural oils. They can also be dried in a low-heat oven. Peppers are best dried by tying them to a string and hanging on a sunny wall or in a covered space. Tomatoes can be sun-dried but, as for the other vetables mentioned above, it is easier to use a small electrically-heated tray dryer. We purchased ours from The Organic Gardening Catalogue. The address is given in Section 4.12.

We find that this is also an excellent way of drying wild mushrooms grown in the garage or under-build.

PART FIVE

PREVENTING AND CONTROLLING PROBLEMS

Problems caused by gales, fluctuating temperatures, frost, hail, starvation, drought, weeds, pests, diseases and animals can all be largely prevented and controlled by simple natural, ecological and organic methods.

5.1 PHYSICAL PLANT PROTECTION

In some locations crops will need some form of protection from hot and cold drying winds, frosts, flooding, animals and birds. Some practical solutions are suggested below.

Protection from hot and cold drying winds

Reduce the exposure of small vegetable growing areas by placing pots and raised beds behind fences or hedges and, if necessary, providing overhead shade during the middle of the day for any young and the more thirsty types of plants, and watering more regularly.

Full-scale vegetable plots are best located in areas of the garden protected by boundary hedges, fences or tall trees. But ensure that the plot is not in the shade for more than a few hours each day.

Within the plot the most vulnerable plants can be sheltered by: low internal fences; tall lines of climbing beans, leaving the cane frame and dead plants of the last maturing beans to provide a winter wind break; rows of sweet corn; Jerusalem artichokes; sunflowers and sweet peas, which also attract beneficial insects; leaving the row of the late-maturing butter bean plants in the ground after harvesting as the dead foliage still gives fair protection through to March.

Even a low 15cm-high fence on the windward side of a row of lettuces can have a significant effect on the line of plants immediately downwind. Likewise, a V constructed with two large prickly pear cacti segments or mini walls of large stones can provide valuable local protection to young melon or courgette plants.

A poly tunnel or greenhouse is also useful for growing out-of-season crops and raising early plantlets.

Early season protection from frosts and to raise temperatures

We use a combination of the following to protect early planted plantlets and recently planted seeds.

a. Cut-off water bottles as cloches for individual plants such as melons and cucumbers.

b. Square plastic-covered frames made from off-cuts of wood over carrots, radishes and young leaf crops sown in early winter.

c. Squares of plastic draped over two arches of strong wire or pliable prunings from fruit trees when planting squashes and melons directly into the ground.

d. Tall cloches made from longer wooden off-cuts covered with plastic sheeting fixed with screwed strips of wood or large drawing pins. The former are the more durable. Useful for any crop grown from seed and early planted tomato plantlets.

e. Tunnel cloches of any length constructed by running lengths of plastic through two arches at say 1.5-metre intervals are useful for many crops.

f. Cold frames are useful for starting off melons, courgettes, squash and pumpkins and the first phase of hardening off plantlets from a heated greenhouse. These can be simply a wood frame covered with plastic or a proprietary three-tiered mini greenhouse.

g. Straw around celery plants.

h. Fleece laid over early planted spring potatoes or potatoes in the ground just before Christmas.

i. Grow early plantlets from seed in a heated greenhouse.

Protection of summer leaf crops from the hot summer sun

Once summer temperatures rise above 28 degrees C leaf vegetables such as lettuces, rocket and spinach soon mature and go to seed. This can be delayed to some extent by erecting a shade over these crops or growing on the west side of the house. Shades are easily constructed using woven polypropylene green or brown windbreak/shading material. This is available in rolls in many garden centres and ironmongers'. Containers and tubs can be protected using old beach umbrellas.

Protection from flooding

The best solutions are to slope the plot so that it does not flood, or surround the vegetable garden area with a wall high enough to prevent the highest level of expected flood waters, plus a bit more, from entering the vegetable growing area.

Protection from animals and birds

The main problems you may meet are:

a. Trampling, digging up and fouling of crops by cats and dogs. Possible preventive solutions include: using Cat Off or Dog Off products around the edge of the vegetable plot — don't put the gel nearer than 50 centimetres from the outside edge of the plot; constructing an electric fence — versions available especially for small animals; fencing in the vegetable plot.

b. Rabbits. We see the occasional rabbit but have never noticed any attack on our crops, probably because we work on the plot most days and because of the availability of wild plants in the area. However, if you do notice serious damage, wire mesh fences with the bottom buried 20 centimetres in the ground are probably the only solution, unless you are a registered hunter.

c. Pigeons can develop a taste for newly sown peas, beans and sweet corn and smaller birds for smaller shallowly sown seeds. Cover the seed beds and young plants with a bird net held 10-20cm above the ground on twigs. Alternative bird-scarers are old CDs on string, old nylon fishing line with strips of silver foil attached strung between two posts and scarecrows with things attached that blow around in the wind.

d. Mice can dig up pea and broad bean seeds in the autumn to build up winter food stores, often in a warm compost heap. They can also burrow to steal a few shallow potatoes and forming peanuts. If this becomes troublesome, set a couple of traps or have a cat (but that could lead to problem 'a' above).

e. In some rural areas rats attack maturing sweet potatoes in the weeks before they are harvested in the late autumn. If the damage is serious, set traps.

f. Wild boar come down from the hills foraging for food, especially during the autumn and winter months. They tend to dig up and eat sweet potatoes, Jerusalem artichokes, potatoes and peanuts. If you anticipate such visitations, make several scarecrows dressed in unwashed clothes (renew human smell occasionally with urine), hang nets of hair (obtained from the hairdresser) on posts around the plot, or fix very strong fences that go 30 centimetres into the ground. Wire mesh fencing is best fixed above a low block wall as boar often burrow under less secure fences. You can also try a two-tiered, low electric fence.

g. In some forest areas deer can be a problem. The only real solution is high fences — they can learn to jump low ones. You can also try the bags of hair as for wild boar.

5.2 PLANT SUPPORTS

Many fruit-bearing vegetables require supports to prevent wind damage, to expose all parts of the plant to the sun to stimulate flowers and fruit and ripen the fruits, and to make harvesting easy.

The vegetables requiring supports and the type of support they need are listed below. Nearly all supports are constructed from canes joined by wire or string ties.

a. Peas: best supported on the twiggy prunings of fruit trees traditionally termed pea sticks. Short, metre-long sticks for medium-height peas and one-and-a-half-metre sticks for tall-growing varieties including mangetout. Sometimes it is possible to purchase seeds for climbing peas, which can require two-metre cane supports, especially some of the heritage varieties.

b. Climbing butter beans: best supported on a two-metre-high tunnel frame as beans form within the mass of leafy growth. This makes it easier to find all the flowers — they need their tips pinching out to stimulate large pods — and to harvest all the beans. The supports for individual plants can be smaller canes than the main tent frame or string tied between two or three horizontal canes on either side of the frame.

c. Other climbing beans: best supported on two-metre high wigwams or tent frames. Again use cane or string supports. In exposed positions reinforce the frame with guy ropes.

d. Tomatoes: best supported on one-and-a-half-metre-high tent frames.

e. Peppers and aubergines: best supported on strong individual canes, or preferably (if you have sufficient canes) by a single-line box frame 70 to 100cm high.

f. Padrón peppers: as they are smaller than large fruiting sweet peppers, best supported in a two-row box frame 60-70cm high.

g. Hot peppers: best supported as for tomatoes.

h. Cucumbers and gherkins: best supported with a box frame a metre high with several horizontal supports.

i. Sunflowers: tall growing varieties can be supported on strong canes but they grow well unsupported.

j. Sweet peas grown to attract pollinators: support as for climbing beans. They grow too tall for pea sticks.

One can use up many canes each summer. Luckily canes last several seasons in the Spanish climate as tall strong canes are often difficult to purchase and when located are often relatively expensive.

The best thing is to grow your own cane plantation if you have a large property, or make friends with a villager who has excess for his needs. Many will probably be glad that you offer to cut out the ripe canes as many rot away as the number of Spanish families actively growing vegetables in large quantities diminishes.

Establishing your own cane plantation is easy. All you need to do is to knock a line of green, un-dried canes into the ground and keep them damp. It is possible to harvest canes within three years and the number will increase each year. Choose the situation for your plantation well as they spread each year.

Canes are normally harvested in January when the moon is waning. The lunar calendar we described in Section 4.15 always indicates the best date/s.

5.3 SUPLEMENTARY FEEDS FOR GROWING PLANTS

There are four approaches to providing the nutrients essential for the growth of home grown vegetables. They are illustrated in the charts below.

APPROACH	PLANT FEEDING PROCESS	END RESULT
A. Don't improve impoverished soil in any way	Roots take in the few nutrients they can find	Unbalanced insufficient food leads to stunted unhealthy plants
B. Enrich soil before sowing/planting	Roots absorb nutrients according to needs at each stage of growth	Steady unforced natural growth from germination or planting to harvest
C. Rely only on occasional feeding with manufactured inorganic liquid or solid fertilisers	Hungry roots take in the unexpected food at above-natural rates when nutrients are available	Too much fast feeding results in forced large vegetables which may attract pests, diseases
D. B plus controlled natural supplementary feeds for more hungry plants	Roots take in nutrients according to their needs at each stage of growth	Balanced diet leads to healthy unforced growth from germination or planting to harvest

If you enrich your soil along the lines of Section 4.3 before planting, you will only need to use supplementary feeds to sustain the nutrient level.

a. Regular supplementary feeds are recommended for:

Summer crops: hungry summer fruit crops, tomatoes, peppers, aubergines, beans, squashes, melons etc.

Winter crops: nitrogen-hungry winter leaf crops, especially lettuces, spinach, chard and brassicas.

b. When you use supplementary feeds do try and use natural/ecological/biological/organic fertilisers and soil-improvers where possible. We prefer to use slow versus fast-release versions. There are now plenty of commercial products available and several homemade fertilisers are easy to prepare, as illustrated below. Fast-release or immediately available plant boosts tend to be extracted too readily and gross, non-tasty, unhealthy vegetables can result.

The types of natural supplementary feeds we use	Examples of why and how we use each	How we prepare liquid feeds and apply dry material
Liquid comfrey and fresh comfrey leaves from plants we grow around the vegetable plot*	**a.** Rich in potassium/potash and contains significant amounts of nitrogen and phosphorus. **b.** An excellent organic fertiliser for all crops but especially fruiting vegetables such as tomatoes, peppers, aubergines, cucumbers, pumpkins and raspberries. **c.** It also stimulates the extraction of essential trace elements from the soil. **d.** We use it as a liquid feed or as a leaf mulch around plants to help retain moisture and eventually add more nutrients to the soil. **e.** Dry leaves are best used by mixing into the compost heap to enrich it.	**Method 1** **a.** Use opaque plastic drum or barrel, preferably with a tap near the base. **b.** Keep in a shady place. **c.** Raise up on bricks so that you can place a container under the tap. **d.** Make a sack out of an old sheet or muslin to fit in the drum and fill with freshly cut leaves (about 1kg of leaves to 10 litres of water). The sack works as a filter to stop the tap from becoming clogged, also easing removal of spent leaves. **e.** Cover with water. **f.** After two weeks the smelly liquid can be used as a liquid feed. Add 250ml to 5 litres of water in a watering-can. **Method 2** **a.** If you don't have a tap make a small hole at the base of the drum. **b.** Pack the drum tightly with freshly dampened cut leaves but do not add any extra water. **c.** With this method it is most important to keep the drum in the shade so that the leaves stay moist and rot down. **d.** Keep a container underneath the hole to collect the black liquid when it starts to drip. Add only 50ml to 5 litres of water. Method 1 needs to be used within 6 months whereas M Method 2 will keep almost indefinitely.
Liquid nettle made from plants harvested from locations not treated with weedkillers.	**a.** It is rich in nitrogen and an excellent organic fertiliser for all vegetables, especially leaf vegetables such as spinach, kale, lettuces, etc. **b.** It encourages strong growth from the seedling stage to harvesting and helps combat diseases and pest infestations. **c.** Once fruit plants are established do not overfeed with nitrogen as they will produce too much leaf and not enough flower.	**a.** Prepare as Method 1 of comfrey above. **b.** For a general feed use dilution of 200ml to 5 litres of water and as a foliar feed 50ml to 5 litres of water. Nettle is very potent so always dilute well.

The types of natural supplementary feeds we use	Examples of why and how we use each	How we prepare liquid feeds and apply dry material
Comfrey/nettle mix	**a.** As both comfrey and nettle contain important beneficial ingredients we mix the two liquid manures to produce a combined feed. **b.** This can also be added to a liquid manure feed.	**a.** Dilute as above and mix.
Liquid manure	**a.** Is a good general feed for growing plants and can stimulate early crops. **b.** Nutrients have already been broken down so plants can benefit immediately. **c.** Manures vary in strength: Strongest, pigeon; strong, poultry, goat, sheep and a compost made up of combined manures including green manures; medium/ low, horse, cow, rabbit and composted kitchen waste. **d.** Liquid manures benefit crops in their early growth but as they near maturity are not necessary. **e.** Exceptions are crops that continue fruiting over a long period e.g. tomatoes, peppers, aubergines, pumpkins.	**a.** Set up drum or barrel as for comfrey, Method 1. **b.** Place only well-decomposted manures and water in the barrels in the following quantities: **Strongest –** I bucketful to 6 of water. **Strong –** 1 bucketful to 4 of water. **Medium/low –** 1 bucketful to 3 of water. The feed will be ready for use in a couple of days. **c.** If you dilute further with 1 part of fertiliser to 2 parts of water in a watering-can, you can feed and water the vegetables at the same time. The weaker the better. Four weekly feeds will be better than one strong monthly feed. A principle similar to homeopathic medicine.
Rich well-rotted compost	**a.** It is a well-balanced feed for all crops especially if it contains animal and green manures such as comfrey and nettle. **b.** Always use well-decomposed compost as it will continue to decay in the soil and encourage disease and unwanted pests.	To give an extra feed mulch plants with a thin layer of compost and hoe in lightly. Also helps to reduce water evaporation.
Ecopark compost without added ingredients	Composted green waste. As well as containing important nutrients for growing all types of vegetables, it adds beneficial humus to the soil.	Mulch around plants helps to add extra nutrients, retain moisture and keep the soil light and workable.
Seaweed harvested when still wet after being swept on to local beaches by storms. Not dried seaweed from further up the beach which is too salty	**a.** Seaweed, high in nitrogen and potash, is good source of minerals and trace elements including iodine. **b.** Especially beneficial to asparagus, root crops such as potatoes. beetroot, the bean family and cabbages. **c.** Add small amounts to compost heap to enhance nutrient content.	**a.** Use fresh as a thick winter mulch on the asparagus bed. **b.** Compost for several months before using as a mulch around crops. **c.** To compost, interlayer 0.25m of seaweed and 0.25m of soil, dampening each layer and covering with an old carpet to keep moist. Don't allow to dry out as it won't rot down.

The types of natural supplementary feeds we use	Examples of why and how we use each	How we prepare liquid feeds and apply dry material
Ecopark compost including composted seaweed.	As above but also good for lightening heavy soils due to its general compost and sand content.	Mulch around plants helps to add nutrients, retain moisture and keep the soil light and workable.
Wood ash	**a.** Produced by burning mature wood, it is high in minerals especially potash. Bonfires with other green materials are of lesser value. **b.** We use it for feeding root crops as it encourages healthy strong roots.	**a.** Collect and keep in a dry place until needed as once it gets wet the minerals leach out. **b.** Sprinkle finely over vegetables using an old sock. If it rains, reapply. **c.** It will add valuable nutrients to the compost heap if sprinkled over the various layers.
Chicken manure	**a.** Contains many plant nutrients but most of all nitrogen which is beneficial to all vegetables, especially tomatoes and leaf crops. **b.** Can also be used as a liquid manure (see above).	**a.** Manure from chickens kept under cover in our area usually consists of mixture of left-over grains and their bedding of rice husks — it needs to be left at least a year to rot before use. **b.** Alternatively, collect dried droppings from your own hens, beat them to a fine powder, mix 2x1 with fine soil or wood ash. Spread finely among crops once or twice a month.
Tomato compost	Very high in humus and beneficial to the healthy growth and fruiting of tomato plants.	**a.** When cropping is over collect disease free leaves, stems and overripe fruit and mix with damp soil in a wooden box and cover. **b.** Leave to decompose until Spring then use as much around next year´s tomato plants.
Bone meal	**a.** A good natural general slow release fertiliser. **b.** Use less than before coming to Spain as difficult to obtain and other alternatives available.	Sprinkle over soil once a year.
Blood	**a.** More readily available in powder form (Sequestrene) than in liquid. **b.** Excellent for tomatoes and peppers.	Sprinkle over soil once a year or use a liquid feed as the fruits start to form.
Dried neem cake **	Residue after crushing neem kernels and seeds to extract the valuable oil.	**a.** Apply as for bone meal. **b.** Also helps control slugs.

Notes: *Comfrey, *consuelda* -(continues on next page).

This herbaceous perennial is well worth growing in a corner of the garden or vegetable plot. The best variety to plant is Bocking 14 Russian comfrey (symphytum-x-uplandicum), which unlike other varieties does not self seed everywhere. You only need a few root cuttings to start as they soon multiply and can be split each year. Our original seven small cuttings have now become several hundred plants surrounding our vegetable plot.

We use comfrey in the ways listed below since it is three times as rich in potassium as most farmyard manures. It also has a good nitrogen, phosphorus and trace mineral content, plus irritating hairy leaves and stems. The comfrey roots go very deep to extract these nutrients from the sub-soil, which the roots of most vegetable plants don't reach.

- Laid with compost at the bottom of trenches prepared for planting beans and potatoes. We also wrap each seed potato in comfrey leaves to prevent scab.
- We prepare liquid feeds, especially for fruit vegetables, as explained in the table above.
- We add comfrey to compost heaps at several levels as an accelerator and to add nutrients.
- A line of plants around our vegetable plot to deter snails. Not totally effective but it does help. It would also be beneficial to plant comfrey around citrus trees.
- Circles of leaves can be used around young seed beds and young plantlets as a second line of defence against snails. When the leaves rot they fertilise the surface soil.
- We also use the leaves to mulch along rows of raspberries and other soft fruits, tomatoes and peppers.

In Spain comfrey plants will normally die back between December and the end of February. They are best split in November or March. In most situations the leaves can be harvested three to five times a year. To yield well the plants need to be kept damp. They benefit from a nitrogen feed — with chicken manure for instance — every spring.

Plant new root cuttings 30cm apart in rows or blocks.

If you have difficulty in obtaining them in Spain, you can purchase them from the following suppliers by mail order: www.OrganicCatalogue.com: www.edwintucker.com; comfreyplants@hotmail.com; and www.chilternseeds.co.uk (this firm stocks seeds of the sister comfrey plant Symphytum officinale, which has a nutrient content similar to Bocking 14. Unfortunately, it flowers and seeds profusely so quickly spreads, therefore not recommended unless you have a large property).

**Neem cake, what is left after neem seeds are cold-pressed. It can be sprinkled on the soil around vegetable plants or mixed into seed beds to give some protection against insects and slugs as well as acting as a slow-release general fertiliser. The only Spanish supplier we know of is Trabe, www.trabe.net. It is also available from the German supplier Niem-handel, kontact@niem-handel.de or www.niem-handel.com.

5.4 WORKING THE SOIL

The main reasons for working the soil.

a. To turn over and break up the soil on a long-unused plot when first starting your vegetable growing. This is best achieved on a small plot by double digging, on a medium-sized plot with a rotavator and on a large plot with a hired plough followed by harrowing or rotavating.

b. To work in organic matter before planting, best achieved by harrowing it into a previously dug small plot and rotavating it into larger plots. During the growing season soil can be maintained and further improved by:

- Spreading organic matter on the surface of unplanted areas during the winter and, when well-weathered, work into the soil.
- Spreading compost/manure on the surface and cover with an old carpet or heavy plastic sheet for a few months until the worms have worked it into the soil.
- Building up no-dig beds by repeating the above every year for three or four years but with alternate layers of compost, swept-up deciduous leaves, manures and shredded soft garden waste. Harder materials are better processed in the compost heap. Gradually you will build up a thick layer of very rich soil where the hungriest moisture-loving vegetables can be planted. This does not work as well in Spain as in northern Europe on a long-term basis due to the continuously hot sun and infrequent rain. We have therefore dug over or rotavated no-dig areas every three or four years. This method is best for building up the worm population in your soil.
- Laying compost/manure in planting trenches for potatoes and beans. Also prepared holes for melons, squashes and pumpkins.
- Spreading compost/manure on the surface of an asparagus raised bed each autumn after cutting back the drying growth. Preferably top the manure layer with a cap of storm-swept seaweed or composted seaweed/garden rubbish compost.
- Working compost/manure into the shallow soil of new seed beds.
- Mulching around the stems of larger vegetables.

c. To de-compact the surface and aerate the upper layers of the soil.

This is best achieved with a swoe (two-sided hoe) followed by a harrow tool. The benefits are that it will reduce the surface evaporation that occurs through the capillaries that develop in the hard crust of compacted and sun-baked earth, allow the earth to breathe and take in oxygen and absorb irrigation and rain water.

d. To kill and remove weeds using a hoe, swoe, mattock or hand fork.

e. To aerate the top 20 to 30cm of soil on a continuous basis (best achieved by building up a worm population, see Section 4.3). In dry weather, dampen the soil first.

5.5 CONTROLLING WEEDS

Whether growing your vegetables inorganically or organically, some weeds are inevitable. If you are growing inorganically, weed-killers can help when first preparing the vegetable plot and if used continuously but sparingly around the plot. However, they also kill off valuable micro organisms and worms in the soil and therefore we only use non-chemical methods. Also in the huerto around the village the use of weed-killers is not allowed once persons start to irrigate via the open water channels. So what can be done? If you are a fanatic for a totally tidy garden, then weed the vegetable plot several times a week and compost the weeds. But this can be time-consuming, especially in the spring when weeds as well as vegetable seeds germinate and grow profusely. Most gardeners, including ourselves, want to take a more laidback or comprehensive approach to the problem and even take advantage of the beneficial properties of some common weeds. We suggest the following:

1. Recognise and accept that weeds are inevitable and that keeping them totally under control — except when growing vegetables intensively on a small scale — may be counter-productive.

2. Control your enthusiasm for a weed-free plot.

3. The first priority is to remove weeds adjacent to shallow-rooted crops such as lettuces and onions or blocks of plants such as young carrots. If you leave the weeds, they compete for moisture and food and eventually for space. But, to avoid unearthing young seedlings, wait until the seedlings have put down firm roots and weeds are large enough to grasp easily.

4. Shallow-rooted weeds around established deep-rooted plants can provide shade for the tops of roots and reduce water evaporation.

5. The second priority is to remove deep-rooted perennial weeds. These are difficult to remove when they mature and, if bits of root are left in the ground, they re-grow and compete with deeper-rooted vegetables, seeding profusely.

6. The third priority is to hoe off the grass and weeds in unplanted areas. Having done this, we either cover them with a layer of well-rotted manure and an old natural carpet and leave the worms to prepare an enriched seed bed over the next three months or plant a green manure crop (see Section 4.7).

7. When we take the carpet off to prepare a seed bed, we first harrow and rake and then leave for a week for any seeds to germinate. We then hoe again before planting. Seed beds can be de-weeded using a flame gun or infrared burner. However there is a danger of killing off useful micro organisms and shallow worms.

8. The planting of seedlings through holes in plastic conserves water and also stops most weeds from growing. However, use a heavy grade of black plastic as thin plastic lets a degree of light through and weeds can grow under the plastic, eventually pushing it up.

9. Put all weeds except deep-rooted perennials on the compost heap. Once rotted down they can be recycled as compost. The final compost will include the minerals and trace elements that weeds took from the soil plus carbon taken in from the air as carbon dioxide during photosynthesis. So weeds become a useful crop.

10. Recognise that some weeds (out of place self seeded wild plants) have additional uses. Borage plants are good for attracting pollinators, marigolds for attracting black fly and fennel flowers for attracting a variety of insects from other plants and larger insects that devour the smaller ones. Horsetail and nettles are so important to us both as a fungicide and nitrogen-rich fertiliser that we cultivate patches on the edge of our vegetable plot.

11. Biodynamic gardening institutes suggest that useful weed inhibitors/killers can be prepared by burning weed seed ash at different periods of the lunar/cosmic calendar. For information contact, in Spain, rudolfsteiner@teleline.es and, in the UK, bdaa@biodynamic .freeserve.co.uk.

12. If you want to try an organic low-risk weed killer try a five-per-cent solution of vinegar, the strength of many vinegars sold for home use. It works best on young weeds and higher strengths would be required for larger deep-rooted perennial weeds, so dig them out.

13. Burn deep-rooted persistent perennial weeds, especially if they have seed heads.

5.6 COMPOSTING VEGETABLE WASTE AND WEEDS FOR RECYCLING TO THE SOIL

What is a good compost?

A sweet-smelling, loamy soil rich in water-retaining humus, plant nutrients, beneficial micro organisms and a worm population produced by the natural aerobic decomposition of green kitchen and garden waste.

What are the benefits?

Compost is an invaluable soil improver in Spanish gardens. It adds natural nutrients, minerals, beneficial micro organisms, worm eggs and humus to the soil or potting composts.

The humus improves the openness, fertility, aeration, lightness, water retaining and drainage properties of the soil to which it is added and overall makes the soil lighter to work. This is of benefit to all Spanish soils, especially if they are clayey or sandy, naturally infertile or overworked, or have for some years only been fed with chemical fertilisers.

During the long hot summer days a rich friable soil will lose less moisture through capillary evaporation than a hard-baked poor soil. And, most importantly, there is evidence that plants grown at a natural rate in a healthy compost-enriched soil can be less prone to disease than fast, weak growth.

Composting is a convenient way of disposing of kitchen and garden waste, including shredded material from the winter cutback in the flower garden.

When can it be made?

At any time of the year from daily kitchen waste, garden prunings and weeding, with a big boost at the time of the winter cutback in the flower garden when all the prunings can be shredded to add to the compost heap.

Why bother?

There are several benefits, even to the small-scale grower.

a. It is a convenient ecological way of recycling green waste back into the soil, especially the daily kitchen waste and the many sacks of shredded material that result from each year's winter cutback in the flower garden.

b. Small, enclosed, tidy, largely odourless composters are now commercially available so that even apartment-dwellers can compost their daily kitchen waste and droppings from the canary cage.

c. It reduces the municipal costs for disposing of household and garden waste and reduces the number of plastic bags used.

d. You can produce a less expensive and better-quality compost than many commercial brands or the compost produced by municipal eco parks.

What materials can be composted safely?

Most green waste material and old newspapers — we discuss this in detail a little later in this section. We do not compost meat or fish waste as it can smell, can add non-beneficial bacteria, and attract insects and rodents.

What types of composters can be used?

Good compost can be made in a number of types of composters, both purchased proprietary and homemade. The most commonly used ones are described in the table opposite.

Type of composter	Capacity for adding material for composting	Speed of composting process	Cleanliness	Cost to purchase or make and in time expand	Ease of expansion without buying a second unit
1. Proprietary wormery e.g. Wiggly Wigglers worm factory**	Small	Very high	High	Medium	Low
2. Homemade wormery using old glass fibre water tank	Small to medium	Medium to high	Medium to high	Low	High, just find another's tank
3. Small proprietary composting bins e.g Bokashi composter**.	Very small	High	High	Medium	Low
4. Multi-trayed composter with large worm population e.g. Wiggly Wigglers Can-O-Worms unit**.	Medium	Hign	Hign	Medium	Low
5. Plastic-lidded composting bins as issued by some local councils free or at subsidised price.	Medium	Medium	High	Low to medium	Low
6. Proprietary wooden or plastic solid-sided composting boxes	Medium to large	Medium	Medium to high	Medium to high	Low
7. Proprietary rotary or tumbler composters of various designs.	Medium	High to very high	High	Medium to very high	Low
8. Homemade wire mesh and post composting box.	Medium to large	Medium	Medium	Low/ medium	High with little cost
9. Homemade from old wooden pallets or doors with wire mesh front.	Medium to large	Medium	Medium	Low	High with little cost
10. Dug out composting pit covered with soil or tarpaulin	Medium to large	Low to medium	Low to medium	Low	High with little cost
11. Pile of material above ground covered with tarpaulin or thick black plastic.	Medium to large	Low to medium	Medium	Low	High with little cost

** Supplied by Wiggly Wigglers (www.wigglywigglers.co.uk)

Wormeries nos. 1, 2 and 4 are easy to keep provided you don't overload them and don't let the composting material become too wet or acid.

Composters type no. 3 give few problems provided you use the recommended accelerators.

Enclosed plastic-lidded composters no. 5 are tidy and work best if some garden waste is mixed in with kitchen waste. Compost accelerators can speed the process. Bottom doors make removal of finished compost easy.

Rotary and tumbler composters type no.7 work most productively if filled with a mix of dry and moist material and regularly turned. Said to be good for grass cuttings. Best if compost accelerators are added.

The box type composters nos. 6, 8 and 9, whether purchased or home made, are the best means of composting large amounts of shredded garden waste but need special attention in Spain due to the generally dry climate. We outline below the procedure we have found to work best and now use on a line of five homemade compost boxes.

Pits no. 10 can work but the hole needs digging out and also the finished compost. Box composters are easier to work and extend.

Compost piles no.11 do not compost well in Spain due to the dry climate.

Success factors for compost boxes

Whether you use compost bins, or have just a heap in a corner of the garden, all will eventually rot down with the help of heat, moisture, oxygen, micro organisms, insects and worms. Just let nature take its course — but there are a few tricks to the trade, especially in the Spanish climate.

Listed are the factors we have found contribute to the making of good compost, speedily and hygienically.

1. Design of the composting boxes

As already explained, proprietary bins or well-operated boxes are essential in Spain, as the open compost heap many gardeners use in rainy northern Europe would soon dry out in the hot Mediterranean climate.

We therefore suggest that you construct two or three composting boxes of the following dimensions: width, depth and height a minimum of one to one-and-a-half metres as it is difficult to build up essential heat at the heart of smaller boxes. Two boxes are better than one as during the process of composting one needs to turn the decomposing material. A third box would allow you to start a second heap while the first is maturing.

A homemade box can be easily constructed by using four posts and wire netting or three old pallets. The front is most easily closed with a wire-netting gate or removable wooden slats for ease of access. To increase aeration use a 10-15cm layer of broken twigs as the base or a fourth pallet. It is best not to place the frame on a concrete base as you need to encourage small insects, worms and micro organisms from the soil into the heap.

2. Positioning of compost boxes

The compost heap needs to retain moisture and build up heat. Ideally it should be situated in a semi shaded corner of the garden.

3. Line the box and cover

To retain moisture and internal heat, line your box with cardboard from old cartons or thick layers of newspaper as you build up the waste materials. Don't make air holes as you would have done in northern Europe as this will only result in the rapid drying-out of the outer layers. Keep the top covered with a layer of damp newspapers topped with a square of old carpet.

4. Layering the different raw materials

Don't just throw waste materials into the bin willy-nilly. If you do, the decomposition will be patchy and essential heat not built up. Build up the heap layer by layer as follows:

a. Start with a 15cm layer of coarse, twiggy material to create air circulation and help start the aerobic decomposition process.

b. 10–15cm of manure or half-decomposed compost. This will attract worms and essential micro organisms.

c. 10–15cm of green waste.

d. 10–15cm of brown waste.

e. 4 sheets of wet newspaper laid over the top. Worms love it, but avoid colour-printed pages.

f. 10–15cm of manure.

g. A sprinkling of wood ash.

Repeat c to g, adding natural accelerators (discussed below) to the layers until the compost box is full.

5. A good mix of raw materials, including:

- **Green waste:** vegetables, fruit (avoid citrus fruits or skins as they are too acidic), crushed egg shells, weeds, soft green cuttings and prunings, grass cuttings, non-diseased leaves and stems of vegetables that have finished cropping, dampened and torn-up paper packets, newspapers, cardboard in centre of toilet rolls and kitchen towel rolls. Don't use cooked kitchen waste, cheese, oil or raw meat, fish etc. as it may attract vermin and flies in the height of summer.
- **Brown waste:** dry fibrous materials such as shredded hard prunings, branches and cuttings, flower heads, stalks, dry leaves, waste from a vacuum cleaner, animal and human hair. It is preferable not to add cuttings from bay, conifers, acacias and oleanders as their residues can be toxic to other plants.
- **Wood ash:** a little will add valuable potassium and lime.
- **Manures:** horse, sheep, goat, rabbit, chicken and pigeon. Stack the latter two to rot down separately as they are very strong, and then only add in small proportions.
- **Accelerators:** seaweed, comfrey, borage, dandelion and nettle in leaf or liquid form are all good accelerators, as well as adding essential nutrients to the heap. The liquid forms can be prepared by steeping leaves in water for two or more weeks. If you don't have access to any of the above, use sulphate of ammonia or a proprietary powder. Human urine is also very effective!
- **Water:** essential for the whole process.

6. Moisture control

Dampen each layer, where necessary, as you build up the heap. This is the best time to add your prepared liquid accelerators. There is no point in leaving material dry as it won't rot down. But don't over-soak as it will then become slimy, stick together and smelly since anaerobic rather than aerobic decomposition will start to take place. It is just a matter of trial and error.

7. Temperature control/decomposition

It is important to line and cover the heap to build up the temperature necessary for bacterial action. Ideally the centre of the heap will build up to 50 to 60 degrees C to kill off weed seeds etc. It will still decompose at lower temperatures, but at a slower rate. Two forms of decomposition can occur within a compost heap:

- **Aerobic:** fast, requiring oxygen. If the heap is well mixed with dampened materials, it will fully decompose in six to 12 months.
- **Anaerobic:** slower and smelly. Material in the heap often becomes slimy and compacted as a result of being over-wet. The solution is to turn the heap, at the same time layering in new dry materials.

The aim is to achieve a totally aerobic process, but even in the best there will be odd corners of anaerobic decomposition taking place.

8. Turning

It is advisable to turn your heap after four to six months to re-aerate it. Prepare an empty bin as for starting a heap. Then fork over the decomposing heap to the empty bin, mixing any dry materials on the outer edge into wet compost in the centre. Remove the lower part if it is ready to use. It should be fine and sweet smelling.

At this stage you top up the partially composted material with fresh materials, and then repeat the process in four to six months' time.

9. Worms

Worms play an important role in the compost heap. Firstly they eat damp waste material and excrete processed waste as very fertile worm casts, and secondly their burrows aerate the heap. They will be attracted by the heat and dampness, but do add in any you find around the garden and always put back any found in the finished compost. They will leave the compost if it is too dry.

10. Potential problems and solutions

Rats: don't include any raw or cooked meat, fish, cheese, oil or salads dressed in oil.
Flies: always top kitchen waste with a layer of dry materials and cover.
Ants: in a drying heap ants will look for moisture in the form of retreating worms. Your worm population is valuable so find where their trail is coming from and put down ant powder.

11. Be patient

One is always short of compost in the vegetable and fruit gardens. But don't try and take a shortcut by using the heap before it is fully decomposed, unless you are using it only for mulching or preparing bean and pumpkin trenches.

5.7 ECO PREVENTION AND CONTROL OF PESTS AND DISEASES

The main problems you may experience are, in general terms, attacks by insects and fungal diseases.

Insects either eat leaves (e.g. slugs and caterpillars), extract sap from leaves or stems (e.g. aphids and red spider mite), attack roots (e.g. carrot fly and wire worm), or eat the fruit (e.g. larvae of pea moth).

Fungal diseases cause leaves, fruit, roots or entire plants to rot off. For example: mildew on the leaves of courgettes, neck rot on onions, club root on brassicas and bottom-end rot on tomatoes. Attacks by insects can be treated with insecticides and fungal diseases with fungicides, but it is better to try to prevent the outbreaks in the first place.

Eco prevention and control aim to grow healthy plants that are less likely to be attacked by pests and diseases by taking practical non-chemical precautions and controlling problems if and when they occur in natural ecological ways.

Our experience is that major problems do not arise with plant pests and diseases provided you grow them naturally and on a multi-cropping versus single-crop basis. Which is what one does in a typical vegetable plot or raised bed. Don't assume that every possible disease and pest is waiting to attack. They won't be, unless you are extremely unfortunate and ignore good practice. So don't rush out in anticipation and buy the wide range of insecticides and fungicides on display in your local garden centre or agricultural cooperative.

But do ensure that you follow the basic good practices outlined below.

A. Some basic good practices

- Don't sow diseased or infected seeds.
- Only plant out strong, healthy plants.
- Don't force-grow weak plants by over-watering and feeding or by using excessive amounts of growth stimulators. See section B.
- Grow a diversity of vegetables in close proximity rather than large areas of single crops.
- Season-by-season crop rotation, as explained in section E below.
- Companion plant beneficial plants, as explained in section C below.
- Provide appropriate physical protection.
- Timely planting of vulnerable seeds. For instance, sow all peas when the weather cools off but before Christmas and perhaps after the field mice have gone into hibernation. That way they can be harvested in April before the weather heats up and there are problems with mildew.
- Pick off and squash beetles and caterpillars when first seen.
- Spray against aphids as soon as first seen or even spray brassicas earlier in their growing season as a precaution.
- Only use eco/organic sprays. Homemade or purchased proprietary are equally acceptable. In some cases purchased sprays may be more concentrated than homemade ones.
- Make a couple of scarecrows with flapping arms to ward off birds.
- Allow your vegetable plot to develop as a balanced self-sustaining ecosystem as discussed in section C below.
- Recognise that most problems will be minor and that the loss of a few beans, lettuces or tomatoes is likely to be insignificant compared to the quantities of unaffected healthy vegetables. So why spray everything, as occurs commercially where every tomato is profit at the expense of every fruit receiving a chemical or at best an eco-spray.

B. Growing naturally

By this we mean growing vegetables at a natural pace so that at each stage in their life cycles the plants are strong and healthy rather than weak, slow-growing plants, caused by a lack of water and poor nourishment, or over-watered and over-fed giants, grown at an unnatural rate and often lacking in flavour, aroma and bite. To grow strong healthy plants select good seeds appropriate to your micro climate and apply good husbandry.

C. Growing ecologically

Under this heading we include the following:

a. Minimising problems by preventing the

buildup of diseases and pests in the soil without using chemicals.

Within this context we include avoiding problems by not growing in the same part of the plot for two years or more the types of vegetables prone to diseases and pests that can build up in the soil. Such plants include brassicas, which are prone to club root, carrots (carrot fly), potatoes (blight and eel worms) and onions (fungal diseases). This can be achieved by operating a form of crop rotation, considered in section E.

b. Minimising problems by not planting antagonistic plants adjacent to each other and by co-planting vegetables that have a positive effect one to the other. See section E.

d. Co-planting beneficial flowering plants that do not impact the growth of vegetable plants

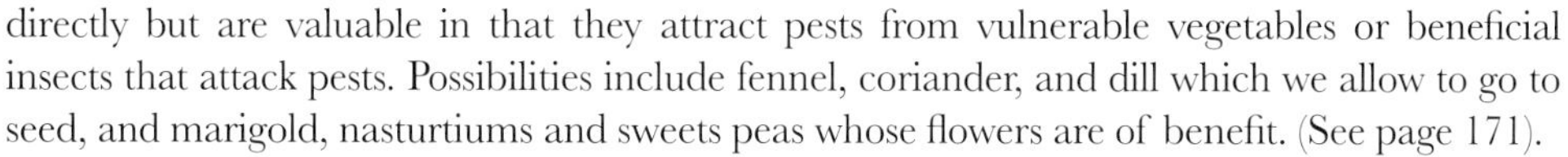

directly but are valuable in that they attract pests from vulnerable vegetables or beneficial insects that attack pests. Possibilities include fennel, coriander, and dill which we allow to go to seed, and marigold, nasturtiums and sweets peas whose flowers are of benefit. (See page 171).

e. Purposely planting "sacrificial insect-attractive crops" that are not our favourites for eating in order to attract insects away from otherwise tempting types of vegetable. For instance, planting sweet corn, the variety grown to feed animals, to attract shield bugs that would otherwise attack leafy vegetables.

f. Physical barriers including mesh fences 40-50cm high around carrots to deter the low-flying carrot fly.

g. Non-chemical deterrents to snails and slugs. A table in section G summarises some possible methods we have used and our current favourites without resorting to purchasing expensive nematodes.

h. Attracting beneficial lizards and toads by building dry stone walls or heaps of rocks near the growing area.

i. Constructing a small pond near or within your vegetable-growing area to attract frogs and toads. It is one of the best ways of reducing the population of slugs and large insects.

D. Growing organically

We have found it possible to avoid using any synthetic inorganic chemical treatments for pest and disease prevention. Instead, to supplement the type of actions already mentioned, we use a variety of sprays using naturally occurring or specially grown plants, or proprietary bio/eco/organic products for evaluation as alternatives for gardeners not interested in making up their own. They are described in section F.

The purchased product that we have made most use of is neem oil, which has an even wider use in controlling pests on fruit trees.

E. Crop rotation

Crop rotation is a concept of most benefit and ease of application on large vegetable plots and with the ten-tub system as outlined in section 3.9. Sections 4.5 to 4.8 indicated the different soil conditions required by different groups of plants. This can be summarised as follows (for convenience we refer to the types of vegetables as R1, R2, F1, F2, FL and L and use these codes in the crop rotation plan chart):

Type of plant	Typical vegetables in group	Soil fertility requirements
Root type R1	Potatoes	High, can tolerate partialy decomposed manure/compost
Fruit type F1	Tomatoes, peppers, squash, melons	High, but with fully decomposed organic materials
Fruit type F2	Beans, peas	High, normally prepared manure/compost-filled trenches or holes for beans
Flower type FL	Globe artichoke, broccoli, romanesque	As F2
Leaf type L2	Lettuce, cabbage, spinach, chard	Medium, but high in nitrogen
Root type R2	Carrots, beetroots, onions, garlic	Medium, dislikes partially decomposed compost/manures

It therefore makes sense to design your vegetable plot as a number of strips, oblongs or squares and prepare one of them especially for each one of the above groups.

However, there is another related phenomenon. If you grow such vegetables as cabbages, potatoes, carrots and onions in the same soil year after year, diseases and pests can build up in the soil, e.g.:

- Eelworms can eat the tubers of carrots, potatoes and other root crops.
- Blight can attack both potatoes and tomatoes.
- Micro organisms can breed, causing brassica plants, especially cabbages, to develop club root.
- Fungal white rot on onions can become a serious problem after a few years.

So it makes sense not to grow each group of vegetables in the same soil on a continuous basis. The most practical solution is to move all the groups of crops after each sowing/planting season whether autumn/winter or spring/summer to new soil on a rota basis.

To allow growing some crops twice a year and as many more vegetables can be grown in Spain during the winter than in northern Europe, we operate the following pattern of crop rotation. Our 800 square metres of land is split into nine five-metre-wide strips bounded by raised ridges since we have nine water inlets from the channelled water distribution system. We use three strips for permanent asparagus, soft fruit and comfrey/herbs/companion plants. In the winter we need less space for growing vegetables as expansive plants such as squash and melons are not grown. The spare area is therefore planted with a green manure such as alfalfa and phacellia or covered with a cap of well-rotted compost or manure and then an old wool carpet. By the spring worms will have worked the organic matter into the top centimetres of the soil and we have the beginnings of good seed beds for the spring.

The chart below illustrates the general pattern of movement of crops. We say general because it does not always work so scientifically. Cold spells can cause over-wintering crops to grow and mature more slowly and later than expected so they have to stay in the ground longer than planned. If we have an exceptionally warm autumn so that good growing temperatures continue to the end of November or even into December, it is possible to continue harvesting fruit crops such as tomatoes and Padrón peppers until those times. Indeed, to exploit the potential of a good autumn, we now sow more seeds ready to plant out six weeks after we plant our main crop of plantlets. Thus, vegetables that follow may have to be slotted in on an area provisionally reserved for a green manure or any other convenient space.

TYPICAL CROP ROTATION PLAN

YEAR	GROWING SEASONS	GROWING AREA						
		1	2	3	4	5	6	7
ONE	Autumn/winter	R1	R2	L	FL	F2	GR	P
	Spring/summer	F1	R1	R2	L	FL	F2	P
TWO	Autumn/winter	F2	GR	R1	R2	L	FL	P
	Spring/summer	FL	F2	F1	R1	R2	L	P
THREE	Autum/winter	L	FL	F2	GR	R1	R2	P
	Spring/summer	R2	L	FL	F2	F1	R1	P

Rotation is more difficult if you have a small plot or raised bed crop. In any case the area of soil is so small that eelworms and problem micro organisms can easily migrate to where their target vegetables are planted. So just follow the good practices suggested previously. Watch out for problems and treat them as they occur. Plants that are strong and healthy are less likely to be attacked and, if they are, can shrug off the attack without major damage to your crops. So avoid over-watering and over-feeding!

Some form of crop planning is required to ensure that you maximise the benefits of co or inter-cropping vegetables with beneficial relationships and that you avoid antagonistic relationships.

The most important ones to bear in mind are as follows.

SOME BENEFICIAL RELATIONSHIPS TO EXPLOIT

1. Onions and garlic around blocks or rows of carrots can deter any lurking carrot flies.
2. Tomatoes planted among asparagus can deter asparagus beetles.
3. Leaf crops benefit from being planted after crops of peas and beans which will have built up the nitrogen in the soil.
4. Climbing beans can be grown up the stalks of sweet corn.
5. Parsnips like beans so co-plant with dwarf beans.

SOME ANTAGONISTIC RELATIONSHIPS TO AVOID

1. Tomatoes do not like being planted next to potatoes as blight can transfer.
2. Garlic, leeks and onions should be kept away from any fruit crops as their smell which is beneficial in deterring unwanted pests can also deter beneficial pollinating insects.
3. Sweet corn dislikes tomatoes and sunflowers.
4. Pumpkins dislike potatoes although they need similar soils.
5. Aubergines dislike being planted alongside tomatoes so plant among dwarf French beans and squash.

A complete list of beneficial and antagonistic plant relationships is provided in the *Companion Planting Chart,* published by www.ecodesignscape.co.uk.

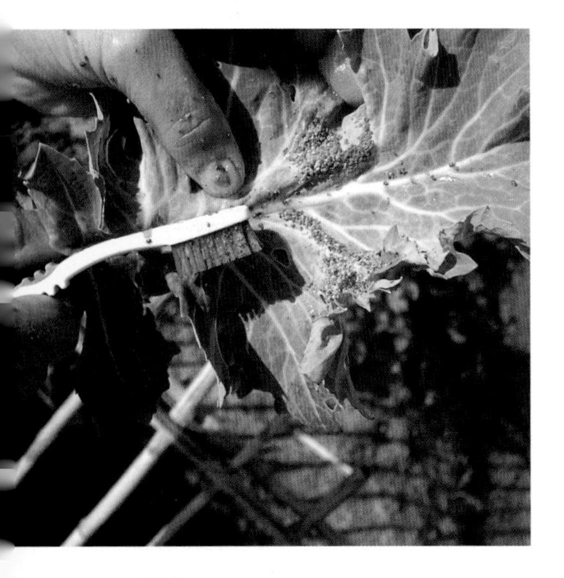

F. Some insect controls and fungicides should you need them

The table below presents ways we have used in recent years to avoid and combat the various pests and diseases you may experience when growing vegetables. We cannot claim they are 100 per cent solutions, but with the preventative actions already discussed the result is that we have no serious problems.

The only proprietary product we have listed is neem, but there are now many other eco/bio/organic solutions generally available should you not wish to spend the time preparing homemade sprays. If you decide to use proprietary insecticide, pesticide or fungicide products, it may help to take an infected leaf or vegetable to the local agricultural cooperative.

Most common Spanish vegetable garden pests and diseases **English** *Spanish* Botanical	**Main plants affected and how**	**What to look for**	**Causes**	**Suggested ecological treatments based on our personal practices**
Asparagus beetle *Criocera de espárrago* Crioceris asparagi	Lay eggs on young asparagus shoots and later on foliage. Adults feed on shoots and foliage	Small black and orange beetle with six square white patches on back on young shoots or summer foliage	Natural attractor	**a.** Pick off. **b.** Interplant with a few tomato plants in spring. **c.** Spray with solutions of potassium soap, nettle or neem
Ants *Hormigas* Lasius niger	**a.** Attack red worms in compost heap. **b.** Remove newly planted seeds, e.g. carrots, radishes	Trails in compost heap or seed beds	Looking for food and moisture	**a.** Find nests and pour hot water down holes. **b.** Keep seedbeds moist at all times. **c.** If your containers, raised beds or vegetables are close to the house or a garden electricity point plug in an electronic ant deterrent unit. NB. Ants can also be beneficial as they feed off aphids.
Aphids *Pulgones* Aphis	Aphids feed by sucking the sap out of plants, especially young plants and those in greenhouses.			General: Maintain a patch of nettles alongside the vegetable growing area to attract ladybirds.
a. Greenfly	Beans, roses, artichokes.	Tiny sticky green insects on stems, leaves and buds. Usually ants feeding off them.	Natural attractor. Too much nitrogen producing fleshy plants.	Spray twice weekly with solutions of potassium soap, nettle or neem.
b. Whitefly *Mosca blanca*	Broccoli and other brassicas.	Tiny white insects covering plant with sticky substance.	As above	**a.** As above. **b.** Interplant French marigolds as an insect repellent. **c.** Hang yellow bottles along lines. (Swill bright yellow paint in a 1.5 litres empty water bottle). They dislike the yellow glare.
c. Blackfly *Mosca negra*	Broad beans, spinach, artichokes	Tiny black insects on upper tips and stems of broad beans. Base of stems of spinach. Flower heads and stems of artichokes	Natural attractor	**a.** Pinch out tops of broad beans when first beans have formed. **b.** Spray twice weekly with solutions of potassium soap, nettle or neem. **c.** Inter-plant spinach and chard with mint in pots to deter flies. **d.** Feed with liquid seaweed to develop stronger, more resilient plants. **e.** Plant a basil plant at the end of the row. (Keep shaded and well watered).
Bean and pea weevils *Gorgojos* Stitonia lineata	Peas and beans. Holes in pods and eaten fruit	Maggots inside pods	Natural attractor	**a.** Rotate crops yearly. **b.** Remove and burn any badly affected plants.
Cabbage white butterfly *Mariposa blanca*	Lay eggs on leaves of cabbages and other brassicas	White butterflies nearby caterpillars eating leaves	Natural attractor	**a.** Pick off eggs and caterpillars daily. **b.** Sprinkle wood ash over plants. **c.** Spray twice weekly with solutions of potassium soap, nettle or neem. **d.** Spread cut sage between rows regularly as a deterrent.

Most common Spanish vegetable garden pests and diseases **English** *Spanish* Botanical	**Main plants affected and how**	**What to look for**	**Causes**	**Suggested ecological treatments based on our personal practices**
Cabbage root fly *Mosca de raíz* Delia brassicae	Flies lay eggs at base of stems of mainly cabbage, Brussels sprouts and cauliflower. Maggots attack roots	Like a common house fly. First sign of damage is when leaves start to wilt and then die off	Smell of carrots attracts flies	**b.** Plant healthy strong plantlets. **c.** Don't plant deeper than in seed boxes. **d.** Don't earth up. **e.** Cut out 10cm slit square of carpet, carpet underlay or cardboard and fit round base of stem to stop flies laying eggs. **f.** Remove and burn any affected plants.
Carrot fly *Mosca de zanahoria* Psila rosae	Flies lay eggs in the holes where plants have been thinned. Larvae feed on roots	Flies with black wings and brown head and yellow legs about 10cm long. Foliage turns red and then yellow and finally wilts. Small holes and maggots in roots	Smell of carrots attracts flies	**a.** When weeding or thinning disturb as little as possible. **b.** Surround with planted onions, garlic or leeks. **c.** Interplant a couple of small rosemary plants and put cut sage in between rows. **d.** Enclose in 75cm high mesh fence - carrot flies are low flying. **e.** Sprinkle powdered seaweed along rows
Chafer beetle *Escarabajo sanjuanero* Melontha vulgarisi	The adult beetle attack roots of plants.	Fat curved white larvae, usually found in the compost heap	Natural attractor	**a.** We leave them in the heap to help with decomposition or **b.** you can remove and drown them.
Colorado beetle *Escarabajo de la patata* Leptinotarsa decemlineata	Eat leaves of potatoes and aubergines	Striped fleshy orange and black bugs. Also yellow patches of eggs	Natural attractor	**a.** Pick off beetles and squash. **b.** Wipe off any newly laid eggs. **c.** Could try a dilute neem spray.
Eelworm *Aguilula (nematodos)*	Mainly affects potatoes. Distortion of buds and leaves and nodules on roots	Microscopic worm like. Difficult to detect	Natural attractor	**a.** Remove and destroy. **b.** Don't grow crops in same place for several years.
Grasshoppers *Saltamontes* Several varieties from small to locusts	They can eat greenery but in our experience they haven't been a problem	Jumping grasshoppers in mid to late summer	Natural habitat	**a.** Catch them if you can or leave them to the frogs. **b.** If you have a real plague ask local agricultural cooperative what eco spray they recom-mend. **c.** A neem spray can help.
Pea moth *Oruga cigarrera* Cydia nigricana	Caterpillars bore into pods	When you open pods you will find peas eaten by small maggots	Natural attractor	**a.** If they are sown in late autumn they should crop before the moth lays its eggs. **b.** Spray crops and soil with neem fortnightly as a precaution.
Shield bugs *Chinches* Palomona prasina	Appear in mid to late summer eating leaves of plants. They can be beneficial as they eat other unwanted insects	Triangular shaped green bugs. Others orange and red	Natural habitat	**a.** Pick off and squash. **b.** Let fennel and coriander plants seed. Bugs congre-gate there rather than eat plants.

Most common Spanish vegetable garden pests and diseases **English** *Spanish* Botanical	**Main plants affected and how**	**What to look for**	**Causes**	**Suggested ecological treatments based on our personal practices**
Slugs and snails *Babosas y caracoles*	Eat young seedlings & damage fruits of melons, courgettes, lettuces, artichokes, raspberries, strawberries, redcurrants	Eaten leaves. Slimy snail trails and missing plants	Natural attractor	**a.** At night with torch remove. **b.** Put down beer traps. **c.** Surround young plants with comfrey leaves or neem cake*. **d.** Spray around plants with garlic solution or neem.
Spider mite *Araña roja*	*Curcúbitas* and vines. Feed off underside of leaves.	Yellowing and blotchy leaves. Tiny spiders with silk-like webs covering underside of leaves.	High tempe-ratures. Too much nitrogen.	**a.** Where possible wipe off. **b.** Twice weekly spray with solution of potassium soap, nettle or neem.
Wireworm *Gusanos de alambre* Agriotes	Attack roots of newly planted peppers, tomatoes and aubergines. Also potatoes, sweet corn, strawberries and carrots.	Hard, thin, slow-moving, shiny-shelled, wormlike larvae. Plants suddenly wilt and die.	Natural attractor	**a.** Crop rotation prevents the problem building up. **b.** Add a little sulphur to fertilisers to improve hygiene of soil. **c.** We haven't had a problem and accept them. If you use liquid ground insecticide, you will kill off red worms, which are invaluable workers of the soil.
FUNGAL DISEASES				
Mildew *Mildiu*	Takes food from plants and interferes with growth.			A neem oil or extract of propolis foliar spray (5ml per litre of water) can be used for all mildew/fungal problems.
a. Downy mildew	Tomatoes, onions, roses.	Pale yellow blotches on leaves.	Damp condition and high temperatures	**a.** Don't wet plants when watering. **b.** Tomatoes – twist 10cm length of copper loosely around the base of the stem and earth in the ground. **c.** Feed liquid seaweed to develop stronger plants which are more resilient.
b. Powdery mildew *Oidio blanco*	Curcúbitas, tomatoes, cucumbers, peppers, aubergines vines and onions	White powdery film on surface of leaves.	As above	As a and c above plus **d.** Fortnightly dust plants lightly with sulphur using a sock. In winter dust vines once or twice.
Botrytis botritis *(podredumbres)*	Tomatoes, onions and garlic	Rotting of leaves, stems and fruit which become covered with grey fungal growth	As above	As above plus **e.** Remove any badly affected plants and fruit

Most common Spanish vegetable garden pests and diseases English *Spanish* Botanical	Main plants affected and how	What to look for	Causes	Suggested ecological treatments based on our personal practices
FUNGAL DISEASES				
Neck rot caused by Botrytis fungi *Podredumbres de cuello*	Weakens onion and garlic plants	Rotting off of seedlings, and necks of bulbs in ground and stored bulbs	Hot damp conditions	**a.** Don't overwater. **b.** Ensure good drainage. **c.** Rotate crops yearly. **d.** Dilute Neem spray
Potato blight *Roña de la patata*	Potatoes - loss of leaves reducing yield	Dark spots on tips of leaves and mould on undersides. Rotting off prematurely	Damp conditions	As above, plus spray ground before planting with nettle/horsetail infusion
Rust *Roya*	Weakens plants of leeks, garlic and beans	Orange/brown pustules on leaves	Damp conditions	**a.** Don't overwater. **b.** Don't wet leaves when watering. **c.** Spray in spring with infusions of horsetail or Neem
OTHER PROBLEMS				
Bottom-end rot	Tomatoes and peppers resulting in loss of fruit	Circular dark patches at base of fruit.	Under watering and over fertilising	**a.** Water regularly. **b.** Avoid over-feeding when fruits are forming. **c.** Spray ground before planting with nettle/horsetail infusion or Neem
Club root *Hernia de col*	Brassicas, especially cabbages and cauliflowers. Plants unable to take up nutrients and water	Wilting seedlings and young plants. Roots swollen and knobbly. Poor growth	Fungus in the soil caused by high acid and poorly draining soil	**a.** Sprinkle the surface of the soil with lime before planting. **b.** Improve drainage of soil. **c.** Crop rotation

Note: * Neem oil is now widely available in Spain but the only suppliers we currently know for neem cake are www.trabe.net and www.niem.handel.com.

METHODS FOR PREPARING NATURAL SOLUTIONS

INGREDIENTS	HOW TO MAKE	HOW TO USE
Garlic *(ajo)*	A decoction* using 50g of crushed garlic to 1 litre of water. Filter and further dilute with 1.5 ltrs of water.	**a.** An insect control. **b.** Spray plants in full sun for 3 days in a row and repeat as necessary. **c.** To deter snails spray plants and surrounding soil regularly.
Horsetail *(cola de caballo)*	A decoction* using 100g fresh stems without roots to 1.5 ltrs of water or 25g of dried to 1.5 ltrs. Filter, cool and use.	**a.** A general spray against fungal diseases. **b.** Spray plant and soil. **c.** Repeat in 2 weeks.
Neem	Make up as per instructions on bottle.	An insecticide and fungicide (see Section 5.12).
Nettle *(ortigas)*	Liquid manure diluted 20:1 or an infusion* using 25g of dried leaves to 1.5 ltrs. Filter, cool and use.	**a.** An insect control. **b.** Spray whole plant. **c.** Repeat if still signs of infestations.
Potassium soap/ insecticidal soap *(jabón Negro/jabón suave).*	Dissolve 25g in 1 ltr of water. Dilute further if too thick.	**a.** An insecticide. **b.** Spray insects **c.** Repeat as necessary.
Tomato	An infusion** using a handful of leaves to a litre of water.	a. Spray plants against rust. b. Repeat as necessary.

Notes:

*A decoction: bring the ingredients to boil and simmer for 15 minutes. ** An infusion: pour boiling water over ingredients. Leave to stand for 10 minutes. Where possible use non-chlorinated water. Dried horsetail and nettle leaves can be obtained from health shops and local markets.

The above sprays can be used in infected greenhouses as well as in the open air. A number of biological controls using one insect to attack another are also available for use in greenhouses. For instance, phytoseiulius, a predator of red spider mite and encarsia for aphids.

5.8 MONITOR YOUR PROGRESS TOWARDS BECOMING NATURAL, ECOLOGICAL AND ORGANIC

This book provides guidelines for achieving harvests of wonderful, fresh nutrient-rich, disease-and-pest-free vegetables 365 days a year by growing them in the most natural manner possible.

This best practice is summarised in the self-audit questionnaire that follows. We suggest you complete this once a year to assess your progress and as the basis for any changes required in your vegetable-growing practices during the next year or two.

After answering the questions, add up your total score and read the observations below the table. Don't be discouraged if you start with a low score but realise that some simple changes can be made during the next 12 months and commit yourself to doing so.

BEST PRACTICE	HOW WOULD YOU DESCRIBE PERSONAL PRACTICES?	SCORE FOR ANSWER	PERSONAL SCORE
1. Improve the structure and fertility of the soil using only natural/ ecological materials	**1.1** Only use proprietary inorganic chemical fertilisers.	0	
	1.2 Use above plus peat and peat substitutes.	1	
	1.3 Now use some compost and have cut back on the use of chemical fertilisers by half.	2	
	1.4 Use well-rotted manure and compost but may include some non-organic materials.	3	
	1.5 Only use well-rotted manure and compost from organic sources.	4	
	1.6 As above plus the use of seaweed.	5	
2. Self production of the materials used for enriching the soil and producing natural feeds	**2.1** Buy proprietary mixes in bags.	0	
	2.2 Buy in bags but have started a small compost heap.	1	
	2.3 Now have a large compost heap and have reduced what is purchased.	2	
	2.4 Now have two compost heaps, a source of well-rotted manure and use some compost from local ecopark.	3	
	2.5 As above but now have a few chickens, rabbits, guinea pigs and hens that produce useful manures.	4	
	2.6 Have purchased a few sheep and goats that keep the orchard tidy. Now totally self-sufficient from own animals, birds, compost heaps and productive wormery.	5	
3. Feed crops with natural/ecological plant feeds when essential during the growing season	**3.1** Use only proprietary inorganic manufactured chemical feeds.	0	
	3.2 Still use above but have started to use proprietary organic/ecological feeds.	1	
	3.3 Now use mainly proprietary feeds but have started to prepare own.	2	
	3.4 Now use only own produced feeds but not sure that all manure used is organic.	3	
	3.5 As 3.4 with all organic manures and plants but only feed the soil.	4	
	3.6 Have a planned programme for using a variety of own organic feeds as soil and foliage feeds.	5	
4. Use non-chemical methods to control weeds	**4.1** Still use proprietary weed killers extensively.	0	
	4.2 Have started to cut back use and now do some weeding by hand and hoe.	1	
	4.3 Hand pick, hoe, and mulch but still use weed killers in the spring.	2	
	4.4 Hand pick, hoe and compost. Some weeds fed to animals. Rest on compost heap.	3	
	4.5. As 4.4 plus smothering with eco carpets and plastic sheeting.	4	
	4.6 As 4.5 plus prepare biodynamic natural weed killers.	5	
5. Use natural/ecological insect deterrents and pesticides and companion planting for pest/disease prevention and control	**5.1** Still use chemical sprays. No companion planting.	0	
	5.2 80% chemical 20% natural.	1	
	5.3 60% chemical 40% natural, started companion planting.	2	
	5.4 20% chemical 80% natural, and much more companion planting.	3	
	5.5 Only proprietary and some own natural sprays, substantial companion plantings and starting to grow naturally.	4	
	5.6 Only own natural plant sprays and sulphur used but extent very much reduced as natural predators, extensive companion planting and growing naturally solve most problems.	5	
6. Plant ecologically/ organically produced and protected seeds	**6.1** Only use regular seeds.	0	
	6.2 Regular seeds with 20% organic seeds.	1	
	6.3 50:50 organic and regular seeds.	2	
	6.4 80% organic seeds.	3	
	6.5 100% organic seeds.	4	
	6.6 100% organic seeds, 30% own seed.	5	

BEST PRACTICE	HOW WOULD YOU DESCRIBE PERSONAL PRACTICES?	SCORE FOR ANSWER	PERSONAL SCORE
7. Watering and feeding are restricted to the levels required to produce natural sized healthy, tasty, crisp vegetables rather than fast growing water filled giants	**7.1** Aim to and achieve mammoth vegetables but we don't really enjoy eating them and we have problems with pests and diseases.	0	
	7.2 As above but we manage to control diseases and pests.	1	
	7.3 Don't really think about the issue but do produce some tasteless vegetables.	2	
	7.4 Starting to recognise the problem and thinking about making changes. Some already started.	3	
	7.5 As 7.6 but only on some crops.	4	
	7.6 Monitor the needs and effects. Generally reducing the need for supplementary feeds and levels of watering by enriching and improving moisture holding capacity of the soil before planting seeds	5	
8. Development/ management of naturally balanced ecosystem	**8.1** Plot sterile. No worms. No wildlife on plot.	0	
	8.2 Worms appearing. Beneficial wildlife starting to visit.	1	
	8.3 Worms breeding. Frogs, toads and ladybirds resident.	2	
	8.4 Many worms. Snakes in residence. Birds nest nearby. Companion and sacrificial planting working.	3	
	8.5 Plot now a haven for a range of natural wildlife who control, with companion planting all serious infestations.	4	
	8.6 As above but now have a number of sheep and goats that keep the orchard tidy, and all edible weeds plus household waste fed to chickens, rabbits and guinea pigs. We are now self sufficient in manures and composts	5	

Observations on scores:

31-40: You have become a full, competent ecological/organic and natural vegetable-grower.

21-30: You are obviously well on the way to becoming a totally organic gardener.

11-20: You appear to believe in the benefits of organic gardening and are making progress.

0-10: You appear to have no real interest in natural, ecological or organic methods at present. Review what you have against natural, ecological and organic principles. Reread Part One of the book and consider changing over to some natural/ecological and organic practices during the next year.

PART SIX

A BASIC VEGETABLE GARDEN CALENDAR

By month for both mini and large scale vegetable growing.

The calendar starts in September as that is the most practical month to begin growing vegetables in the open ground after the long hot summer. With falling temperatures, it's a good time to start to replant window boxes and containers with autumn vegetables and perennial herbs. For those new to Spain, it is also easier to grow them first during the autumn/winter/early spring before learning to cope with the conditions of late spring and summer. Having said that, gardeners on the high meseta and mountainsides which have heavy winter frosts and snow would be best to start in March. But the autumn is also a good time to gear up your growing of sprouting seeds and enjoy the fruits of growing mushrooms in grow bags wherever you live. If you grow summer vegetables in containers, tomatoes and peppers will obviously still be cropping so it's worth having a few spare containers in which to start off autumn/ winter vegetables.

SEPTEMBER

A. Mini-scale growing

1. Collect suitable containers.
2. Fill with a good compost mix.
3. Buy and plant plantlets for lettuces and sow radishes and cut-and-come-again salad mixes.
4. Purchase a cultivated or wild mushroom grow bag.
5. Start to grow sprouting seeds weekly or monthly.

B. New vegetable plot, raised beds and tubs

1. Decide on the type and size of your vegetable garden and where to locate it.
2. Collect tree tubs or build raised beds.
3. Depending on the size of vegetable plot clear, double dig, rotavate or plough the area.
4. Mix well-rotted manure and compost into the top 15 centimetres of soil.
5. Harrow and rake the soil into a series of ridges and hollows if irrigating by flooding, or rake level if planning to use perforated irrigation tubing.

6. If planning to start on a small scale in containers, or raised beds, fill them with a 1:3 mix of well-rotted manure and compost and a reasonable soil.
7. Collect a pile of manures to rot down for the spring.
8. Sow some green manures on vegetable plot.
9. Cut back main growing shoots on tomatoes to encourage new growth and continuing cropping.
10. Sow lettuce, radish, onion and leek seeds and buy plantlets for lettuces and other salad crops.
11. Collect compost with seaweed from Eco park.
12. Set up watering system.

C. If you have been growing crops through the summer

1. Continue to feed peppers and tomatoes to prolong their fruiting.
2. Harvest and store pumpkins, squashes and melons.
3. Convert excess crops of peppers, tomatoes, onions and courgettes into chutney.
4. Continue to pick out ends of flowering shoots on butter beans to stimulate the formation of larger beans.
5. Autumn cutting of comfrey leaves. Place some in barrel to produce fertiliser and mulch raspberries with remainder.

OCTOBER

A. Mini scale

1. Sow window boxes and containers with cut-and-come-again salad leaves, radishes etc.
2. Plant or replace herbs in window boxes or pots.
3. Plant up containers with plantlets of "wok brok" or sprouting broccoli, onions, leeks etc.
4. Try out some different sprouting seeds.
5. Harvest first mushrooms.

B. Vegetable plot, raised beds and tubs

1. Plant plantlets for winter salad and green crops such as spinach and sea kale beet.
2. Sow seeds for winter root crops — carrots, parsnips, beetroot and radishes.
3. Sprout a few potatoes and plant to produce new potatoes for Christmas.
4. Cut back asparagus bed or plant out new plantlets.
5. Plant seeds of useful companion plants such as marigolds and nasturtiums.
6. Sow the first batch of broad beans, peas and mangetout for the spring.
7. Plant onion, leek, broccoli, cauliflower, cabbage, spinach, sea kale beet and lettuce plantlets and remember to take precautions against slugs and snails.

8. If possible, plant according to the most preferred days in the lunar calendar.
9. Continue to harvest over-summered crops such as carrots, tomatoes, peppers and beans.
If no autumn rains, install an irrigation system.

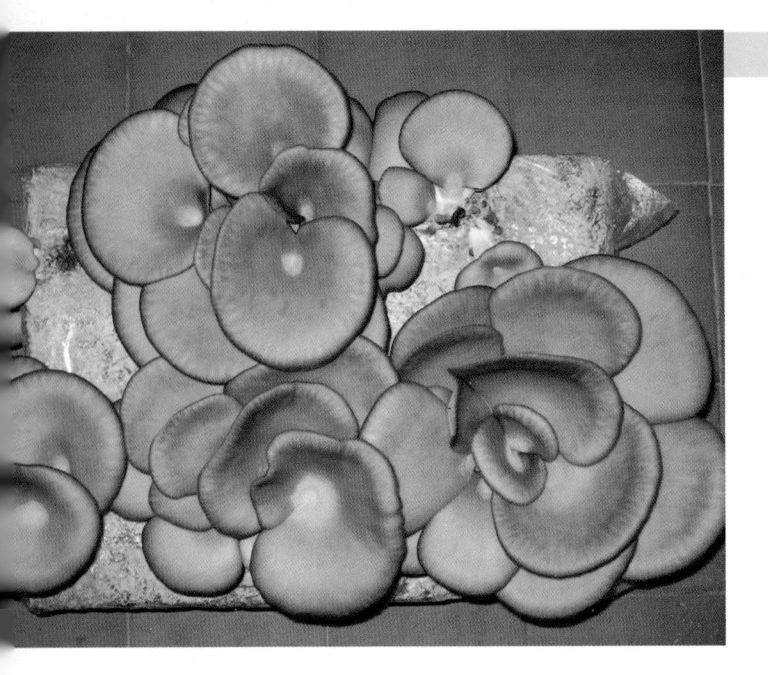

NOVEMBER

A. Mini scale

1. Plant up containers with plantlets if not done last month.
2. Keep cutting cut-and-come-again salad leaves.
3. Empty containers of tomatoes and peppers once they stop producing.
4. Build raised bed in patio garden.
5. Buy a grow bag of another variety of setas to have ready for Christmas.

B. Vegetable plot, raised beds and tubs

1. Plant comfrey plants around the vegetable plot if you can obtain them. If not, do this in the spring. Split existing plants to increase size of crop.
2. Build compost bins.
3. Plant a line of sweet peas as their flowers attract pollinators in the spring and enrich the soil with nitrogen.
4. Sow a second batch of broad beans, peas and onions and also some leeks for planting on in the spring.
5. As summer crops finish, give the plot a good clean-up. Put remains of vegetable plants and annual weeds on the compost heap and have a bonfire for perennial weeds. Don't forget to get a licence first.
6. Earth up potatoes which should be up by now.
7. Harvest the last butter beans, paella beans and young fennel and spinach.
8. Make and put up a scarecrow.
9. Collect together all good used canes and support in a cane rack to keep them dry and strong for re-use next year.
10. Cap any unused areas with well-rotted manure and compost and cover with carpet to produce seed beds for vegetables which like a newly manured soil.
11. Put straw round celery to protect from frosts. Also cover globe artichokes with straw in very frosty areas.
12. Cut back asparagus and cover bed with a layer of seaweed, manure and compost.

DECEMBER

A. Mini scale

1. Grow a festive crop of sprouting seeds for Christmas salads.
2. Plant garlic cloves.
3. Harvest radishes and sow new crops.
4. Thin out carrots and use thinnings for salads.
5. Buy a mini wormery to start to produce own compost.

B. Vegetable plot, raised beds and tubs

1. Make last winter sowings of broad beans and peas. Also plant garlic cloves.
2. Transplant thinnings of beetroots and fennel.
3. Harvest lettuce, rocket, purslane, potatoes, salad onions and chives.
4. Sow some oak-leafed lettuce, carrots, parsnips and beetroot under plastic tent cloche.
5. As soon as sown, sprinkle some dry wood ash and what comfrey leaves you have as a circle around the area sown to deter snails which can be at their most active at this time of year. Also set up other deterrents to slugs and snails as in Section 5.6.
6. Give brassicas a nettle foliar feed, which will also deter any white fly that may be around.
7. Cover newly planted broad bean and pea seeds with protective netting against hungry pigeons.
8. Build a new raised bed and fill with a mixture of fallen leaves, compost, manure and seaweed. Dampen and cover with a carpet or sheet of heavy plastic until February and then plant potatoes as a first year crop.
9. Cap the asparagus bed with ten centimetres of manure and seaweed.
10. Give the plot a good weed when the weather is dry but the soil is damp enough for easy removal.
11. Ensure that all new plantlets and seedlings do not dry out.
12. Check that vegetables being stored, such as potatoes, squash, garlic and onions, are in good condition and immediately remove any that show signs of decay.
13. Reclothe scarecrows with recently worn, old clothes and hang small netting bags of hair on boundary posts to deter wild boars.
14. Dig large planting holes for melons, pumpkins and squash and fill with a mix of well-rotted manures and compost ready for spring plantings.
15. Stick in prunings from fruit trees as pea sticks to give support to pea plants when they take off in the new year.

16. Check that all garden scissors and pruners are in good working order. Oil and change springs and sharpen blades if necessary.

JANUARY

A. Mini scale

1. Construct a 50cm-deep mini raised bed for growing potatoes.
2. Collect rocks and build a snail bed for vegetables and herbs.
3. Collect five old tyres for constructing a tyre bed.
4. Start off tomatoes from seed on warm window-sills.
5. Cut and dry excess crops of mushrooms.

B. Vegetable plot, raised beds and tubs

1. Watch out for and spray black fly on broad beans.
2. Place yellow painted bottles on sticks between brassicas to deter whitefly.
3. If whitefly appear, spray plants with a soap/nettle solution.
4. Cut and put new canes in a drying rack.
5. Support growing peas with twiggy sticks. Long thin prunings from fruit trees are ideal.
6. Dig up rest of winter potato crop before first frost.
7. Look out for seed potatoes and induce them to chit (sprout) in a cool dark place.
8. Sprinkle wood ash around onions and leeks.
9. Plant out more leek and onion plantlets.
10. Give leaf vegetables a nitrogen feed.
11. Give all tools and machines a good cleanup, oil wooden handles and mechanisms and have machines overhauled if necessary.
12. Dig large and deep planting holes for spring plantings of melons, squashes, pumpkins and courgettes, and fill with well-rotted manures.
13. Take preventative measures against marauding wild boar.

FEBRUARY

A. Mini scale

1. Fill newly constructed tyre bed, snail bed and raised beds.
2. In sheltered areas plant up potatoes in a deep, raised bed.
3. Rejuvenate last year's containers by removing a third of the earth and mixing in new compost and worm compost ready for planting up next month.
4. Sow oriental salad mixes in window box, containers or raised beds.
5. Start looking out for early spring plantlets.

B. Vegetable plot, raised beds and tubs

1. Spring clean the greenhouse and garden frame.
2. Turn over last autumn's compost heaps sieving what is nice and crumbly for preparing compost for seed trays and pots for large seeded varieties.
3. Sow trays of lettuce, annual herbs, tomatoes, courgettes, pumpkins and water melons in greenhouse.
4. Plant more onion and leek plantlets.
5. Spray peas with horsetail solution to protect against mildew on pods.
6. Plant potatoes if in a frost-free location. If not, plant in second half of March.
7. Earth up potatoes as the first leaves appear and spray earth with horsetail solution to prevent fungi.
8. Sow more spring crops in greenhouse.
9. Overhaul and improve the irrigation system.
10. Give comfrey a dressing of chicken manure.
11. If a warm spell, harvest the first asparagus.
12. Give broccoli a feed to prolong cropping.

MARCH

A. Mini scale

1. Plant up window boxes with trailing tomatoes, nasturtiums, come and cut again lettuces, herbs etc.
2. Start garlic cloves and onion plantlets in containers.
3. Start children off with a mustard and cress hedgehog.
4. Set up mini automatic watering system.
5. Give all vegetables a light feed.

B. Vegetable plot, raised beds and tubs

1. Sow last squash, pumpkins, tomatoes, aubergines in the greenhouse or cold frame. Also plant pumpkins and squash directly in the ground under plastic cloches.
2. Plant/sow out beneficial companion plants such as roses, borage, marigolds and nasturtiums.
3. Harvest asparagus, peas, mangetout, broad beans, broccoli etc. while young and tasty.
4. Plant another bunch of onion plantlets for summer harvesting and winter storage.
5. Control weeds as the weather warms up.
6. Put down a number of pieces of heavy black plastic, raised on two bricks and kept damp underneath, as a good snail trap.
7. Give a comfrey feed to all fruit vegetables growing on the plot.

8. Tie in vigorously growing sweet peas and tall growing peas.
9. Give artichokes a good soaking and feed with a liquid nettle, manure and comfrey cocktail or a general ecological fertiliser.
10. Keep asparagus weeded during the main cropping period.
11. Plant potatoes when risk of frost has past.
12. Scatter wood ash around onions and leeks.
13. Pinch out tips of broad beans to prevent blackfly.

APRIL

A. Mini scale

1. Plant containers with tomatoes and peppers.
2. Plant tier of window boxes with tumbling tomatoes, salad vegetables, herbs and alpine strawberries.
3. Plant a mini raised bed with carrots, radishes and beetroots.
4. Empty containers of winter brassicas crops and prepare for replanting.
5. Prepare a bumper crop of sprouting seeds for the Easter holiday.

B. Vegetable plot, raised beds and tubs

1. Collect nettles and steep in water for a useful high-nitrogen feed.
2. Prepare cane supports for tomatoes, peppers, aubergines, climbing beans and cucumbers.
3. Plant out first summer salad plantlets and squash, melon, peppers and tomatoes. Protect with plastic cloches if still cold.
4. Make final sowings of carrots,

parsnips and beetroots.
5. Take a first cutting of comfrey and add to barrel.
6. Place comfrey in circles around new planted plantlets and new sowings to protect against snails.
7. Main harvest of broad beans and peas. Freeze the excess while still young.
8. Plant out giant pumpkins, lettuces, artichokes, sweet corn, French beans and runner beans, early tomatoes, water melons and sunflower seeds and plants.
9. Plant herbs such as dill, coriander, basil and parsley in the greenhouse.
10. Dig first spring new potatoes.
11. Watch out for asparagus beetle. Co-plant tomatoes to deter.
12. Try and keep on top of weeds.
13. Select large pods of tasty peas and broad beans and mark them for growing to maturity for next year's seed .

MAY

A. Mini scale

1. Plant dwarf and climbing beans, cucumbers and courgettes in containers or tubs.
2. Harvest young tender garlic planted in March.
3. Ensure all containers don't dry out when the weather warms up.
4. Clear out winter crop of cut-and-come-again salad leaves and re-sow.
5. Watch out for insects and diseases as the weather becomes more humid.

B. Vegetable plot, raised beds and tubs

1. Plant peanuts and the last carrots before the summer.
2. Plant out courgettes, rest of tomatoes, squashes, pumpkins, gourds, melons, peppers and aubergines.
3. Pick out side shoots on tomatoes and tie them to supports as they grow.
4. Weed or hoe beds regularly before they go to seed. Add dampened weeds to the compost heap.
5. Watch out for black fly on artichokes and treat before they get into the heads.
6. Harvest last of over win-

tered onions and garlic and hang up to dry in semi shade.

7. Make successive sowings of climbing and dwarf beans.

8. Sow sweetcorn and plant out sunflower plantlets to provide windbreaks and to support climbing beans.

9. Snails are very active in the spring, especially after watering. So be constantly vigilant.

10. Transplant leek seedlings.

11. Earth up late potatoes as they emerge and keep an eye out for Colorado beetles on leaves.

12. Harvest selected pea and broad beans seeds. Dry and and store for sowing next year.

JUNE

A. Mini scale

1. Start to shade salad crops from heat of day.

2. Harvest perpetual salads to stop them going to seed and prolong their harvest.

3. Dust tomatoes, peppers, cucumbers and courgettes with sulphur weekly.

4. Don't let any containers dry out.

5. Harvest and dry mature garlic.

B. Vegetable plot, raised beds and tubs

1. Plant out cucumbers, gherkins, butterbeans, dwarf beans and last tomatoes.

2. Start to dust the leaves of courgettes, pumpkins, gourds, tomatoes, peppers, cucumbers, beans with sulphur powder once a week and continue until September.

3. Plant broccoli, cauliflower and cabbage seeds in trays to produce plantlets for planting out in the autumn.

4. Clean out broad bean and pea beds when they have finished cropping.

5. Harvest bean and pea pods for seed when dry and further dry in the sun before storing.

6. Increase frequency and quantity of watering as the weather warms.

7. Tie up tomatoes, peppers, aubergines, climbing beans and cucumbers as they grow.

8. Take a second cutting of comfrey.

9. Feed globe artichokes with comfrey to stimulate more edible flower buds.

10. Watch out for blackfly on artichokes and spinach and spray.

11. Tie in climbing beans as they grow.

12. Turn and dampen compost heaps.

13. Thin out fruits on melons and pumpkins to improve size.

14. Prick out ends of butter bean flowers as they form to improve size of pods.

15. Keep on top of weeds.

JULY

A. Mini scale

1. Grow a good mix of sprouting seeds as cut-and-come-again comes to an end in the hot weather.
2. Cut excess herb growth to dry or freeze.
3. Keep up the watering.
4. Keep dusting with sulphur as in June.
5. Remove non-flowering side shoots on tomatoes.

B. Vegetable plot, raised beds and tubs

1. Increase the watering as the temperatures rise and feed plants weekly.
2. Watch out for infestations and spray as soon as seen.
3. Hoe around plants to keep soil loose, weeds under control and reduce capillary evaporation.
4. Dig out any perennial weeds before they flower and put in a heap for burning.
5. Remove any annual weeds before they flower and seed and add to the compost heap.
6. Plant climbing beans for autumn harvest.
7. Don't forget to continue dusting with sulphur.
8. Sow onions, leeks, cabbage, cauliflower, brussels sprouts, broccoli, spinach etc. in seed boxes to produce plantlets for planting out in the autumn.
9. Mulch tomatoes, peppers and aubergines with well-rotted compost to help retain moisture.
10. Check that the compost heap is damp and not drying out. If necessary, turn and water layers with a dilute comfrey solution. Comfrey is a good accelerator.
11. Harvest potatoes as required.
12. Check watering system for blockages and leaks.
13. Keep bare soil hoed to minimise capillary evaporation.

14. Mulch around fruiting plants with well-rotted compost/manure.
15. Start to make chutneys and bottle surplus fruit vegetable crops.

AUGUST

A. Mini scale

1. Harvest onions and dry.
2. Don't forget to keep the bean sprouts going. They grow fast at this time of year.
3. Keep feeding tomatoes and peppers to prolong their harvest.
4. Start to sow salad vegetables for the autumn.
5. Keep salad vegetables shaded from hot sun.

B. Vegetable plot, raised beds and tubs

1. Harvest main crop onions on a good root crop day according to the lunar calendar. Before storing onions dry them for a week in semi-shade before hanging up in bunches or plaits.
2. Harvest melons, pumpkins and squash for storage in a well-ventilated cool place.
3. Harvest red peppers and chillies and hang up to dry for storage and winter use.
4. Pull or dig out finished plants and put stems and roots on the compost heap.
5. Hoe or lightly dig the used beds. Cover with five centimetres of well-rotted compost or manure and then cover with an old carpet or black plastic. The beds should be well-worked by worms for planting in October and November.

6. Keep on top of perennial weeds. Pull or dig them out before they seed.
7. Keep watering and feeding. If you nurse tomato plants they can continue fruiting until November.
8. Remove and pot up any self-seeded tomato plants from flower pots, raised beds or around the compost heap. Put them in the greenhouse to raise tomatoes for Christmas.
9. Start digging up peanuts. Wash the soil off the shells and dry thoroughly in the sun. Store in shells until eaten fresh or baked in a low oven.

10. Up-date your vegetable record chart.
11. If starting a new vegetable plot or planning to enlarge it, clear the area or weeds ready for ploughing or rotavating in September.
12. Review the success and failures of the last vegetable gardening year and prepare a planting plan for the next 12 months from September.
13. Keep feeding Padrón peppers to prolong their harvesting to the end of October/ November.
14. Plant a final crop of tomatoes for autumn/early winter harvesting in fully sheltered situations.
15. Keep an eye on brassicas raised from seed last month.

VOCABULARY AND INDEX

The vocabulary includes the following sections.

The main index commences on page 209

VOCABULARY

MEASUREMENTS

pulgada: inch
pie (.308 metres): foot
metro: metre
área: 100 square metres
hanegada (traditional measurement used in Valencia and other regions): 833.33 square metres
fanega, fanegada (measurements used in Andalusia): 64 areas, 6460 square metres,1.59 acres
hectare: 10,000 square metres acre (.405 hectares or 4047 square metres): acre
arroba: 25 pounds
kilo: 2.2 pounds
1000 kilos, tonelada métrica: metric ton
litro: 1.76 pints
cubo lleno: bucketful

USEFUL WORDS

allotment: *huerto*
basket: *capacho, cesta*
bed, vegetable: *bancal de verduras*
garden: *jardín*
garden, vegetable: *huerto*
garden, fruit: *jardín frutero*
gardener: *jardinero*
bonfire: *hoguera*
climate, macro: *macroclima*
climate, micro: *microclima*
climate, nano: *nanoclima*
cloche, bell: *campana de cristal/plástico*
cloche, tunnel: *túnel - mini túnel de plástico*
companion plant: *planta beneficiosa acompañante*
composter: *compostador*
compost heap: *montón de abono vegetal, pila de compuestos*
container: *contenedor*
copse: *bosquecillo*
diet: *dieta*
disease: *enfermedad*
diversity: *diversidad*
drainage: *drenaje*
drought: *sequía*
fence: *cerca, vallado*
flower bed: *cuadro, macizo, lecho de flores*
frost, air: *escarcha del aire*
frost, ground: *escarcha*
furrow: *surco*
garden frame: *mini invernadero*
gardening, vegetables: *horticultura*
greenhouse: *invernadero*
grow bag: *saco para cultivar*
gutter: *gotera, canal*
hail: *granizo*
hedge: *seto*
hole: *hoyo*
hose: *manguera*
house: *casa*
injury: *herida*
insect: *insecto*
irrigation system: *sistema de riego*
ladder: *escala*
ladder, step: *escalera de tijera*
lawn: *césped*
moon/lunar calendar: *calendario lunar*
mound, earth: *montón de tierra*
mulch: *alcolchado*
nature: *naturaleza*
orchard: *huerto de frutales*
path: *vereda/senda*
patio: *patio*
pergola: *pérgola*
pest: *plaga*
plant: *planta*
plantlet: *plantula*
plant pot: *maceta*
pollination: *polinización*
pond: *estanque*
property: *propiedad*
rain: *lluvia*
rain, to: *llover*
rainwater: *agua llovediza/de lluvia*

raised bed: *macizo elevado*
ridge: *caballón*
rockery: *jardincito*
row: *hilera*
seat: *silla*
seed bed: *semillero*
seed box: *caja de simientes*
shade: *sombra*
shed garden: *cobertizo*
shrub: *arbusto*
shrubbery: *arbustos*
slope, up: *cuesta*
slope, down: *declive*
smallholding with house: *finca*
smallholding without house: *parcela*
snow: *nieve*
strip plot: *huerto estrecho*
sun: *sol*
sun hat: *sombrero*
terrace (cultivated): *terraza, bancal*
tub: *cubeta*
ten-tub vegetable garden: *huerta de diez cubetas*
tie: *atadura*
tools, garden: *útiles de jardinería*
trellis: *enrejado*
vegetable plot: *huerto*
view: *vista*
water: *agua*
water butt: *tina/barril para agua*
waterway, channel: *canal, acequía*
watering-can: *regadera*
wall: *muro*
watering system: *sistema de riego*
weed: *mala hierba*
weather: *tiempo*
wildlife: *fauna*
windbreak: *abrigada, cortavientos*
wormery: *vermicompostador*
worm: *lombríz*
yard: *patio, corral*

MATERIALS

bag: *saco*
basket: *capacho*
bottle: *botella*
box: *caja*
bucket: *cubo*
cane: *caña*
chippings: *gravilla suelta*
compost: *abono vegetal*
face mask,spray/dust: *antifaz*
fertiliser: *abono*
fertiliser, foliar: *abono foliar*
fertiliser, granular: *abono granulado*
fertiliser, soluble: *abono soluble*
fleece: *malla térmica, fleece*
fungicide: *fungicida*
gloves: *guantes*
goggles: *lentes protectoras*
grit: *cascajo, grava*
handle, spare: *manga disponible*
herbicide: *herbicida*
insecticide: *insecticida*
labels, plastic: *etiquetas de plástico*
manure: *estiércol*
mulch: *mantillo*
netting: *red*
peat: *turba*
pesticide: *pesticida*
Ph meter: *contador de Ph*
post: *poste*
rock: *roca*
sack: *saco*
sand: *arena*
seeds: *semillas*
sheet plastic (solid): *hoja de plástico*
sheet plastic (woven): *malla de plástico*
slab of rock: *bloque*
soil: *suelo, tierra*
stake: *rodriga, estaca*
string: *cuerda*
thermometer: *termómetro*
timer: *interruptor horario*
tray, seed: *bandeja de semillero*
water: *agua*
wax: *cera*
weedkiller: *herbicida*
wire: *alambre*
wood: *madera*
worm, earth: *lombriz*
worm compost: *humus de lombriz*

TOOLS

axe: *hacha*
blower/vacuum cleaner: *aspiradora*
broom: *escoba*
bucket: *cubo*
bucket (basket-like): *capacho*
cane: *caña*
chisel: *escoplo*
dibber: *plantador, almocafre*
dryer: *secadora*
duster (see powder blower)
fork: *horca*
funnel: *embudo*
grafting tape: *cinta de injertar*
hammer: *mortillo*
handle, spare: *mango disponible*
harrow: *grada*
hedge trimmer: *recortador de setos*
hoe: *azadón, peta*
hose: *manguera*
knife: *cuchillo*
mallet: *mazo*
mattock: *azadón, pico*
multi-headed tool: *herramienta de multi-cabeza*
pick axe: *pico azado*
pipe, plastic: *tubo plástico*
pliers: *alicates*
plough: *arado*
powder blower: *espolvoreador*
pruners, extendable: *tijeras de podar extensibles*
rake: *rastrillo*
ridging rake: *bilbadora, rastrillo de caballones*
rotavator: *moto azada, retovato*
saw: *sierra*
secateurs: *tijeras de podar*
scissors: *tijeras*
sharpening stone: *piedra de afilar*
shovel: *pala grande*
shredder: *trituradora*
sieve: *criba*
sledge hammer: *mazo*
sock: *calcetín*
stocking: *media*
spade: *pala*
sprayer: *pulverizadora*
sprinkler: *rociadera*
step-ladder: *escalera de tijera*
strimmer: *desbrozadora*
swoe: *azada*
tank: *cisterna*
teaspoon: *cucharilla*
tool: *herramienta*
trowel: *desplantador, palustre*
watering-can: *regadera*
weeder: *escardera*
weed extractor: *extractor de malas hierbas*
wheelbarrow: *carretilla*
water pump: *bomba para aqua*

PARTS OF PLANTS

bark: *corteza*
blossom: *flores*
branch: *rama*
bud: *brote*
bud (flower): *capullo*
bud (leaf): *yema*
cutting: *esqueje*
flower: *flor*
flower head: *cabezuela*
fruit: *fruta*
graft: *injerto*
leaf: *hoja*
perfume: *perfume*
plantlet: *plántula*
pollen: *polen*
root: *raíz*
seed: *semilla*
seed head: *cabezuela*
seedling: *plántula*
spray of flowers: *ramita*
stem: *tallo*
string of onions/garlic: *ristra de cebollos/ajos*
texture: *textura*
trunk: *tronco*
twig: *ramita*

TYPES OF PLANTS

annual: *anual*
bamboo: *bambú*
bulb: *bulbo*
cactus: *cactus*
climber: *trepadora*
corm: *bulbo*
fruit tree: *frutal*
grass: *hierba*
ground cover: *cubierto por el terreno*
house plant: *planta de interior*
herb: *hierba aromática*
palm: *palma, palmera*
perennial: *perenne*
rambler: *enredadera*
shrub: *arbusto*
shrub (climbing): *trepadora*
succulent: *suculento*
tree: *árbol*
tree (evergreen): *árbol de hoja perenne*
tree (deciduous): *árbol de hoja caduca*
vegetable (green): *verdura*
vegetable (general): *hortaliza*
vegetable (pulses): *legumbres*
variety: *variedad*
vine, grape: *vid*
vine, other: *enredadera*
weed: *mala hierba*

GARDENING VERBS

axe: *hachear, dar hachazos*
bloom, flower: *florecer*
brush up: *cepillar*
build: *construir*
burn: *quemar*
bury: *enterrar*
buy: *comprar*
cascade: *caer en cascada*
change: *cambiar*
choose: *elegir*
clean up: *limpiar*
climb: *subir*
connect: *conectar*
cook: *cocinar*
construct: *construir*
cover over: *cubrir*
create: *crear*
cultivate: *cultivar*
cut: *cortar*
cut back: *recortar*
cut down: *talar*
dampen: *mojar, humedecer*
deadhead: *descabezar*
decide: *decidir*
design: *diseñar*
develop: *desarrollar*
die: *morir*
dilute: *diluir*
dig: *cavar*
dig a hole: *excavar*
dig in: *añadir al suelo*
dig over: *recavar*
dig up: *desarraigar*
distill: *destilar*
divide: *dividir*
do: *hacer*
drip: *gotear*
dry: *secar*
eat: *comer*
earth up: *tomar caballón de tierra*
employ: *emplear*
empty: *vaciar*
emulsify: *emulsionar*
enjoy: *divertirse*
fertilise: *fertilizar*
fill in: *llenar, rellenar*
fill up: *repostar, llenar*
flood: *inundar*
force: *forzar*
garden (general): *trabajar en el jardín*
garden (work on vegetable plot): *cultivar el huerto*
graft: *injertar*
grow: *crecer*
hammer: *clavar*
harrow: *gradar*
harvest: *recoger*
hoe: *azadonar*
identify: *identificar*
irrigate: *regar, irrigar*
label: *etiquetar*

level: *nivelar*
line: *alinear*
kill off: *exterminar*
maintain: *mantener*
mark: *señalar, marcar*
maximise: *sacar el máximo partido a*
measure: *medir*
minimise: *minimizar*
mix: *mezclar*
mix in something: *añadir algo*
mow: *cortar*
open: *abrir*
open up: *abrir*
pinch out: *quitar con los dedos*
plan: *planear*
plant: *plantar*
plough: *arar*
pollinate: *polinizar, fecundar*
pour: *echar*
propagate: *propagar*
protect: *proteger*
prune: *podar*
pump: *bombear*
rain: *llover*
rake: *rastrillar*
ridge: *caballonar*
rotate, crops : *cultivar en rotación*
rotavate: *trabajar con motorcultor, roturar*
saw: *serrar*
select: *escoger*
separate out: *apartar*
screen: *tapar*
shade: *proteger del sol*
shake up: *agitar*
sharpen: *afilar*
sieve: *cribar*
shear: *cortar*
shred: *triturar*
shelter: *resguardar*
snow: *nevar*
soak: *remojar*
sort out: *clasificar, separar*
sow: *sembrar*
spray: *pulverizar, rociar*
spread: *extender*
sprinkle: *rociar*
stake: *rodrigar*
start, motor: *arrancar*
stimulate: *estimular*
stir: *agitar*
strim: *desbrozar*
sweep up: *barrer*
take out: *quitar*
thin out: *entresacar*
tidy up: *arreglar*
tie up: *atar*
till: *labrar*
top up: *llenar*
train: *guiar, dirigir*
transplant: *trasplantar*
trench: *excavar*
turn on: *abrir*
turn off: *cerrar*
turn over: *volver*
turn, rotate: *girar*
turn, soil: *volver*
use: *usar*
water: *regar*
weed: *desherbar, escardar, sacar las malas hierbas*
weigh: *pesar*
wet: *mojar*
wilt: *marchitar*

GARDENING ADJECTIVES

colourful: *lleno de color vivo*
bright: *brillante*
burnt: *quemado*
by the hour: *por hora*
chemical: *químico*
clammy: *pegajoso*
clayey: *arcilloso*
cloudy: *nublado*
cold: *frío*
comfortable: *cómodo*
cool: *fresco*
cosy: *acogedor, propicio*
damp, humid: *húmedo*
dappled: *moteado*
dead: *muerto*
dry: *seco*
drying: *secando*

dull: *sombrío*
dying: *moribundo*
early: *temprano*
ecological: *ecológico*
firm: *firme*
flooded: *inundado*
flowery: *florido*
free-draining: *de drenaje libre*
frost-bitten: *congelado*
frosty: *de helada, escarchado*
frozen: *congelado*
going to seed: *granando*
grafted: *injertado*
growing: *creciendo*
healthy: *sano*
heirloom: *reliquia de familia*
heritage: *herencia*
hot (climate): *cálido*
hot (weather): *caliente*
infested: *plagado*
in flower: *floreciente*
in fruit: *con fruto*
juicy: *jugoso*
level: *a nivel*
late: *tarde, último*
liquid: *líquido*
muddy: *lodoso, embarrado*
natural: *natural*
organic: *orgánico/ecológico*
inorganic: *inorgánico*
perfumed: *perfumado, aromático*
powdered: *en polvo*
prickly: *espinoso, con pinchos*
rainy: *lluvioso*
ripe: *maduro*
rotting: *podrido*
sandy: *arenoso*
seasonal: *estacional*
season, early: *temprano*
season, mid: *medio*
season, late: *tardío*
shady: *sombreado*
sharp: *afilado*
sheltered: *abrigado*
short: *corto*
sloping: *inclinado*
spiky: *puntiagudo*
stunted: *enano*
sunny: *soleado*
sub-tropical: *sub-tropical*
tall: *alto*
temperate: *templado*
tropical: *tropical*
unripe: *inmaduro, verde*
young: *joven*
warm: *cálido*
water: *agua*
waterlogged: *anegado*
water supply: *abastecimiento de agua*
watery: *acuoso*
windy: *ventoso*
wilted/withered: *marchito*

VEGETABLE NAMES
(including herbs and companion plants)

alfalfa: *alfalfa*
anise: *anís*
artichoke, globe: *alcachofa*
artichoke, Jerusalem: *tupinambo*
asparagus: *espárrago*
aubergine: *berenjena*
basil: *albahaca*
bean: *judía, alubia*
bean, broad: *haba*
bean, butter: *garrofón, judía*
bean, French climbing: *judía enrame*
bean, French dwarf: *judía baja, frijol, enana*
bean, haricot: *judía tierna, judía blanca, alubia*
bean, runner: *perona, judía trepadora*
bean soya: *haba de soja*
bean, string climbing: *habichuela, judía verde*
beetroot: *remolacha*
borage: *borraja*
broccoli: *brécol, brócoli*
brussel sprout: *col de bruselas*
cabbage: *col*
cabbage, red: *col lombarda*
calabrese (type of broccoli): *calabrese*

c(h)amomile: *manzanilla*
capers: *alcaparra*
cardoon: *cardo, penca*
carrot: *zanahoria*
cauliflower: *coliflor*
celeriac: *apio nabo*
chickpea: *garbanzo*
chicory: *escarola, achicoria*
chili: *chile, ají*
chives: *cebollinos, cebolletas*
chrysanthemum: *crisántemo*
comfrey: *consuelda*
coriander: *cilantro*
courgette: *calabacín*
cress, land: *berro de tierra*
cress, water: *berro de agua*
cucumber: *pepino*
cucumber, melon: *pepino melón*
cumin: *comino*
dandelion: *diente de león*
dill: *eneldo*
fennel: *hinojo*
garlic: *ajo*
ginger: *jengibre*
kale: *berza rizada, col rizada*
kohlrabi: *colinabo*
leek: *puerro*
lettuce: *lechuga*
marigold: *caléndula*
marjoram: *orégano*
melon: *melón*
melon, water: *sandía*
mint: *menta*
mustard: *mostaza*
nasturtium: *capuchina*
okra: *kimbombo*
onion: *cebolla*
onion, multiplier: *cebolla multiplicadora*
onion, spring: *cebolleta*
pak choi: *pak choi*
parsley: *perejil*
parsnip: *chirivia*
peanut: *cacahuete*
pea: *guisante*
pea, mangetout: *cometodo*
peas, sweet: *guisante de olor*
pepper: *pimiento*
pepper, hot: *pimiento guindilla*
pepper, very hot: *pimiento de cayene*
pepper, ornamental: *pimiento ornamental*
pepper, Padrón: *pimiento de Padrón*
pepper, sweet: *pimiento dulce*
peppermint: *piperita, menta, hierba buena*
phacellia: *facelia*
potato: *patata*
potato, sweet: *boniato*
pumpkin: *calabaza*
purslane: *verdolaga*
radish: *rabanito*
rocket: *oruga, jaramago*
romanesque: *romanesco*
rose: *rosal*
rosemary: *romero*
rue: *ruda*
sage: *salvia*
salad leaves, oriental: *salandini, oriental*
sorrel: *acedera*
spinach: *espinaca*
sprouted seeds: *semillas germinadas* (full list in section 2.3)
squash: *calabaza*
squash, butternut: *calabaza butternut or violín,*
squash, turk's turban: *calabaza turks turban*
sunflower: *girasol*
sweetcorn: *maíz dulce*
sweet pea: *guisante de olor*
Swiss chard: *acelga*
tarragon: *estragón*
tomato: *tomate*
turnip: *nabo*
tiger nut: *horchata*
turmeric: *cúrcuma*

INDEX